WALKING
OFFA'S DYKE PATH

Offa's Dyke rising to Herrock Hill, Herefordshire

WALKING
OFFA'S DYKE PATH

A journey through the border country of
England and Wales

by
David Hunter

Illustrations by
David and Vera Hunter

Cicerone Press
Milnthorpe, Cumbria

© David Hunter 1994
ISBN 1 85284 160 5
A catalogue record for this book is available from the British Library

ACKNOWLEDGEMENTS

Acknowledgement is made to the input to this book at many levels by Vera Hunter and to Peter and Shirley Quy who shared some of our adventures. I am also indebted to Jim Saunders, the Offa's Dyke Path Project Officer for his expert assistance.

Advice to Readers

Readers are advised that whilst every effort is taken by the author to ensure the accuracy of this guidebook, changes can occur which may affect the contents. It is advisable to check locally on transport, accommodation, shops etc. but even rights of way can be altered and, more especially overseas, paths can be eradicated by landslip, forest fires or changes of ownership.

The publisher would welcome notes of any such changes.

Cicerone Guides by the same author:
The Shropshire Hills
Walking Down the Wye
Severn Walks

Front cover: Offa's Dyke Path. Broadrock from Wintours Leap

CONTENTS

Note: The division of the route into the component sections is purely arbitrary and permutations permitting shorter or longer days and the planning of round walks are possible. The distances are sub-divided in each chapter to assist such flexibility.

The discrepancy between the mileage for the official route and the suggested route, see Appendix A, is mainly covered by diversions to places of interest and to accommodation centres. It is difficult to reconcile the distance of 168 miles quoted on the commemorative plaque on Sedbury Cliffs with today's route.

DIAGRAMATIC PLAN OF OFFA'S DYKE PATH

Prestatyn

Rhuddlan

St Asaph

Denbigh

Bodfari

Ruthin

Moel Fammau

Bwlch Penbarra

Llandegla

Wrexham

Llangollen

Froncysyllte

Oswestry

Llanymynech

Welshpool

Buttington

Montgomery

Newcastle

Clun

Knighton

Kington

Hay-on-Wye

Pandy

Hereford

Abergavenny

Monmouth

Sedbury Cliffs

River Severn

Chepstow

1: *An introduction to the walk*

In the last quarter of the eighth century, Offa, the powerful king of Mercia and overlord of the greater part of England, constructed a great dyke to mark out the western boundary of his kingdom and to control incursions from Wales. Twelve hundred years later this great linear earthwork, the longest in Britain, became the inspiration for a long distance footpath traversing the border country of England and Wales for 170 miles from Sedbury Cliffs on the River Severn to Prestatyn near the estuary of the Dee. The Offa's Dyke Path, a National Trail funded by the Countryside Commission, generously signed and waymarked throughout, was opened in July 1971. Undertaken in its entirety the route offers an attractive and at times demanding prospect for the long distance walker which should only be undertaken after careful preparation.

If this seems rather too much of a challenge to take up, do not close these pages in despair for all is not lost, you too can share in the adventure. In common with most of Britain's long distance trails the Offa's Dyke Path, or ODP as it will prove more convenient to call it from now on, can be enjoyed in a variety of ways. There are a number of sections that readily facilitate the planning of round walks, the Wye Valley and the Black Mountains are particularly suited to the purpose. You may opt to make your exploration in short bursts, a few days or a long weekend travelling between conveniently accessible points, perhaps completing the whole route over a period of a year or two as opportunity permits and you succumb to Offa's Dyke fever!

The Offa's Dyke Path makes its way through a varied, some times wild, often remote and frequently superb scenery, linked by a succession of historic towns and attractive villages. A broad brush description at this point will serve to put colour on the canvas, the finer details will emerge as progress is made through this wholly delightful border country which has played such an important part in the history of these islands.

It is an intricate weaving of paths, ancient tracks and quiet lanes, sometimes favouring England, sometimes Wales and occasionally a carefully neutral treading of the division between the two, following the spirit if not always the line of the dyke. Diversions are made from its course to seek a more scenic route and indeed there are many gaps where the dyke was never built.

From the south the ODP follows the high wooded cliffs above the Wye but with opportunities to make a closer acquaintance with this, one of our finest rivers. A descent is made from the superb viewpoint of the Kymin to the historic town of Monmouth which even as this book is being written is discovering that it may be even older than had been suspected. A tangle of twisting lanes and field paths thread their way through the rolling sheep pastures of Gwent to reach the foot of the Black Mountains at Pandy. The long passage over the mountains by the Hatterrall Ridge which peaks at around 2,300 feet marks the highest point of the ODP and in good weather, whatever the season, is one of the highlights of the walk.

After the high level trek from Pandy which completes the first fifty miles the walker will enjoy a leisurely browse round the many bookshops of Hay-on-Wye now following a new career as a centre of the second-hand book trade. Gloucestershire, Gwent and Powys have all been visited, now the ODP cuts across the north-western tip of Herefordshire, descending from the 1,400 feet high Hergest Ridge to the Saxon town of Kington and the telling of the horrific legend of Black Vaughan.

Offa's great earthwork, missing from our route since leaving the Wye Valley village of Redbrook, is met again on the way to Knighton, Trefyclawdd - the town on the dyke. From Knighton a long climb above the valley of the Teme provides some of the finest sections of the dyke which reaches its highest point on Llanfair Hill, here the bottom of the ditch to the top of the bank may be as much as twenty feet. The walker is soon passing through the still remote area of the Clun Forest with the path after bisecting the ancient Kerry Ridgeway leading on to Montgomery. By-passed by main roads and time it presents a fine example of a small county town which has changed little over the past two centuries.

The Severn, a very different river from that briefly seen at the start of the walk, is met again some 110 miles on at Buttington. A diversion to Welshpool is made via the Montgomery Canal to enjoy the terraced gardens and rich furnishings of Powis Castle. More leisurely walking by the canal and the Severn leads to Llanymynech with its hill fort and heritage centre. Onward then to a true border town, Oswestry, named for Oswald the Christian king of Northumbria killed here by Penda, an ancestor of Offa, in the battle of AD642.

Llangollen is reached after visiting Chirk Castle and a not unadventurous crossing of the Dee via Telfords famous 121 feet high Pont Cysyllte aqueduct. Llangollen is another place to pause for breath and explore the town, you may wish to visit Valle Crucis Abbey, Plas Newydd home of the "Ladies of Llangollen", the Horseshoe Falls, take a trip on the steam railway or horse-drawn barge or pay your respects to the ancient kings of Powys at Eliseg's Pillar.

On then via the Panorama Walk to Pen-y-stryt and the long trek over the Clwydian Hills, peaking at the Jubilee Tower on Moel Famau at 1,817 feet. The final stretch from Bodfari takes the walker to Prestatyn on the narrow coastal strip of North Wales, with its holiday camps providing perhaps the greatest contrast of the whole journey.

It is troubled territory we tread with a fluid border which has moved with the ebb and flow of a tide governed by the relative strengths of those trying to retain their homeland or rival powers determined to add fresh territory to their dominions. Not one found it an easy task.

Following the Roman invasion of AD43 many of the British put up a spirited resistance. Two names stand out from the history of the times, the first, Boudicca, Queen of the Iceni in the fen country. She led a large army in a fierce attack which overwhelmed Colchester, put London to the torch and destroyed Verulamium, now St Albans, before they were in turn almost annihilated in AD62. A decade or so earlier, Caractacus, the son of Cunobelinus who had ruled wisely and well from his capital at Colchester, had led a strong opposition to the Romans. After inflicting a humiliating defeat on the legions in the Essex marshes, Claudius retrieved the situation, recapturing Colchester and for a time bringing resistance to an end in the south. By around AD50 the Romans under Ostorius Scapula determined to put an end to the resistance which continued along the western borders and to move his armies beyond the Severn. Somewhere in this border region a great battle took place ending in the defeat and eventual capture of Caractacus. The site is not known, speculation has suggested the British Camp set high above the Severn plain on the Malvern Hills, Church Stretton's Caer Caradoc, a similarly named hill to the north-east of Knighton or Llanymynech Hill on today's border and directly on the line of Offa's Dyke.

We skip not a few centuries returning to the period of Mercian domination later. Following the decline of Mercia the often quarrelling Welsh princes found unity under Gruffydd ap Llywelyn who had an unlikely ally in Aelfgar the Earl of the East Angles who had been evicted from his territory. Trouble errupted along the borders with the Welsh raiding Hereford. In AD1055, Harold, later to be King of England following the death of Edward the Confessor, was put in charge of a force sent to intercept the raiders. Further bloodshed was avoided by a truce agreed at Billingsley. The following year the Welsh resumed their raids but a fresh reconciliation was arranged with Edward. The border dwellers enjoyed an uneasy peace but in 1062 Gruffydd launched further raids on England. Harold was again despatched with a force of cavalry, this time to Rhuddllan on the River Clwyd just south of present day Rhyl. The Welsh leader having received news of Harold's advance made good his escape by sea.

It was winter, not the time for a sustained campaign, and Harold wisely contented himself with the destruction of Gruffydd's palace and the burning of his remaining ships. Harold was one of the hard men of his day and did not forget. With the coming of summer 1063 he left by sea from Bristol on a bloody campaign of retribution. The heavy armour of his foot soldiers was discarded, the cumbersome waggon trains carrying supplies which dictated the pace of an army's advance were made redundant. Harold adopted the classic tactics of the guerrilla, moving swiftly, raiding farms and villages for sustenance. The vengeance of Harold must have been terrible to behold; although the Welsh fought with all their old ferocity they were defeated time after time. Every able-bodied Welshman unfortunate enough to find himself in the path of the English was put to the sword. As Gerald of Wales was later to record, at each battle site a stone was erected bearing the legend "Here Harold was

Victorious".

With the conquest of 1066 the Normans came and studded the countryside with their castles, at first the simple earthen mound and timber fort of the motte and bailey. Later as the need arose they built the castles we know today, stone bookmarks in the pages of history. Many of the greatest of these were built in the reign of Edward I as he strived to maintain a hold on the principality.

Llywelyn ap Gruffydd, the last native born Prince of Wales, so often referred to as Llywelyn the Last now comes into the story of the border country. His position was officially recognised by Henry III but on the succession of Edward he evaded taking the oath of loyalty. He was in conflict with other Welsh princes and by 1276 engaged in open warfare with the king's army under the command of Roger Mortimer. Llywelyn was eventually obliged to acknowledge the king's sovereignty and a few years of peace followed. It was not to last long, by 1282, perhaps as the result of an insensitive regime by local administrators Llywelyn and his brother Davydd were in revolt. Llywelyn was killed near Builth, his memorial is to be found at Cilmery.

The years move on and Owain Glyndwr steps to centre stage as he too proclaims himself Prince of Wales. His story is reserved until we advance along Offa's Dyke into what is now called Glyndwr country.

In 1471 Edward IV established the Council of the Marches, sitting at Ludlow and occasionally Shrewsbury, it supervised the affairs of Wales and the border counties for the next 200 years.

The Civil War starting in 1642 brought its own distress to the territory and the end of the era of the castles as the seige cannons and starvation brought down the walls. In the 1840s the Chartist riots resulted in a brief but potentially serious uprising that alarmed the government of the day to the extent that it turned out the militia to deal with the crisis.

This, by no means complete, catalogue of bloodshed and disaster, when it seems that the four horsemen of the Apocolypse were on patrol of these unhappy borders with scarcely a break to return to their stables, is not included just to add drama to the narrative. We shall meet the echoes of these turbulent days as the Marches lift the veil on their story.

Many bridges have been built on the Offa's Dyke Path. Near Monmouth, Gwent

PRACTICAL MATTERS

It is now time to turn to the practical aspects of following Offa's Dyke Path before completing this introduction with a brief history of the rise and fall of the Mercian kingdom.

This book has been designed to allow some flexibility in following the official route. While this is fully described, alternative routes which allow visits to places of interest or to find accommodation are included and form part of the total mileage quoted. Each chapter covers what for some would be regarded as more than a full day's walk. The overall distance has been further subdivided to allow for shorter excursions, a there and back exploration, or to assist in planning round walks.

SKETCH PLANS AND ROUTE DESCRIPTION

The sketch plans which accompany each chapter are not a substitute for the Ordnance Survey maps but should be helpful in following the general direction of the walk and relating it to the OS sheets. A full list of maps both 1:50,000 and 1:25,000 is given in the Useful

Signposts along the way

Information section. In many areas the walker may be content to use the 1:50,000 sheets (1¼ inches to the mile) while the larger scale (2½ inches to the mile) with its greater detail may be preferred for the more mountainous terrain. This in particular requires competence in the use of map and compass in poor visibility.

It will soon become obvious that a great deal of effort has been made in providing stiles, bridging streams, signing at road junctions and waymarking. The waymarks take varying forms: plastic discs, arrows on trees and rocks, Offa's Dyke Path and distances writ large on signposts or quite simply the Countryside Commission's acorn logo. Nevertheless signs fall casualty to wind and weather and the occasional outbreak of vandalism may leave inconvenient gaps. The route description has been made as detailed as seems appropriate, but for much of the way the walker will have no problem in navigating from one waymark to the next with only occasional reference to book and map.

CLOTHING AND EQUIPMENT

Boots with ankle support and good sole grip whose comfort has already been tested are essential for the enjoyment of the ODP for the terrain varies between the grassy paths of sheep pastures, the level tread of towpaths to rough ground broken by tree roots and rocks and the black peat of the wild moorlands.

Let comfort and protection be your first consideration, with layers of clothing that can easily be accommodated in rucksack or backpack rather than a single bulky garment so that you may keep cool when it's hot and warm when it isn't. Headgear should not be disregarded with a cap worth carrying throughout the year; the high open landscape offers little shelter from chill winds. The route has been described south to north for the value it gives in the improving lighting of the landscape but it does mean that in high summer the sun may be on the back of your neck for long periods, in these conditions a sun hat should not be despised.

Wet weather gear does more than keep the rain off and is a useful overall protection from the wind. A survival bag should be carried together with whistle and torch, six long blasts or flashes followed by six short is a recognised distress signal. A small first aid kit for personal use should include adhesive plaster, antiseptic cream, sting relief, insect repellent - if you are susceptible - a roll of crepe bandage, a triangular bandage and sun cream with a suitable filter factor.

Take sufficient food for whatever is planned, plus emergency reserve of quick energy food such as nuts and raisins, mint cake etc. Drink is a heavy item but should not be neglected especially in hot weather.

The day walker will need only a modest sized rucksack, the weekend walker a little more. The experienced backpacker will require no advice from me but if this is a new venture have a practise outing before embarking on a longer expedition. Watch the weight, review your list and reject that which is not essential.

Accommodation should be found without difficulty in the main towns and villages and the increasing popularity of the trail has seen the sprouting of bed and breakfast signs along the route. Please refer to the Useful Information section as part of your advance planning. Advance booking may not come amiss in the main holiday season.

THE RISE AND FALL OF THE KINGDOM OF MERCIA

In the early seventeenth century Mercia could only be counted as an unimportant also-ran in the fragmented kingdoms of these islands. The accession of Penda in AD626 led to a change in the power base and a redrawing of the map. Penda's territory was small but he was an ambitious man and set to with a will to extend his boundaries. He perhaps recognised that in those uncertain days the weak or meek were swallowed up by those who recognised that strength of arms was the best insurance policy for survival.

Two years after Penda's accession he challenged the West Saxons, defeating them in battle at Cirencester. Peace was agreed and Mercia's sphere of influence increased.

In AD633 in a joint campaign with Cadwallon of Gwynedd, Mercia took on the great power of the day, Northumbria, killing its king, Edwin (later canonized), at a battle on Hatfield Chase, Hertfordshire. Penda went on to defeat the East Angles, further extending the territories over which he held sway. The new king of Northumbria, Oswald, would have viewed with alarm the growing threat from Penda. Battle was joined near Oswestry, Penda beat the Northumbrians and Oswald lay dead upon the field of conflict. Penda and his army plundered Northumbria but retribution was to come in AD655 when after a further invasion Oswy who succeeded to the throne in AD651 defeated him near Leeds.

We move on to the Mercia ruled by Ethelbald for the forty-one years from AD716. He too was of a warlike disposition and by

AD731 was effectively the master of all England south of the Humber.

In AD733 Ethelbald successfully took the war to the West Saxons striking deep into Somerset. Seven years later he was following in the blood stained footsteps of Penda with forays into Northumbria. In AD743 in conjunction with the subject West Saxons he was at war with the Welsh. But, like the blackmailer who does not know when to stop, he tightened the screw on the West Saxons to such an extent that Cuthred their king decided that enough was enough. Taking the initiative Cuthred took his people into battle, defeating the Mercians at Burford in the Oxfordshire Cotswolds.

Ethelbald survived, his credibility did not, Mercian power waned and in AD757 he was murdered. Beornraed seized the throne but was quickly removed by Offa who was to rule for thirty-nine years. First he set about stabilising his kingdom then to a steady period of expansion achieved through conquest, political acumen and the arranged marriages of three of his five daughters. In turn the East Angles were beaten into submission, Kent was defeated at the battle of Otford in AD775 and the East Saxons came within his dominion. He conquered the West Saxons at a decisive battle at Benson. He went on to attack the Welsh, acquiring and holding land beyond the natural boundary of the Severn bringing parts of Powys within his domain including modern day Shrewsbury. It was about this time that he defined the boundary between England and Wales with the construction of the great dyke which bears his name.

Despite all this military activity Offa should not be seen simply as a warlord. He was the acknowledged King of the English recognised both by the Pope and the Emperor Charlemagne. He encouraged trade, created a stable currency, and is credited with the introduction of the silver penny and the striking of a gold coin to facilitate trade with middle eastern countries. Offa was generous in his grants to the monasteries: Worcester, St Augustines Canterbury, St Albans, Evesham were amongst those so blessed. He made an annual payment to Rome for the benefit of the poor and to provide candles for St Peters, the origin it is said of Peter's Pence.

There are events baldly stated in the Anglo-Saxon Chronicles which are unexplained, it reports that in AD792 King Ethelbert was beheaded by Offa. The reason it is not clear but speculation may not be out of order. His daughter Elfrida seems to have been promised in marriage to Ethelbert, the King of the East Angles. Could it be that Offa remembered the uprising of the West Saxons that lead to the downfall of Ethelbald and experienced some sort of premonition as Ethelbert visited him at his palace at Sutton Walls near Hereford?

Folklore attributes strange stories to the murder of Ethelbert. Mysterious lights appeared over his grave and a ghostly figure materialised instructing that Ethelbert should be taken to Hereford for burial. The orders of the spectre were duly obeyed, and to this day the cathedral is jointly dedicated to St Ethelbert and St Mary.

In AD795 Offa was again fighting the Welsh. He died in AD796, the beginning of the end of Mercian supremacy, for times were achanging. He was succeeded by his only son Ecgfrith. Offa with an eye to the succession had already had his son annointed as the future ruler but it proved to be an empty gesture for the new king of Mercia survived his father by only a few months.

It was not Ecgfrith's brief reign that was to mark the change, the die had already been cast nine years earlier with the start of the Danish raids. In the following century the initial isolated forays became a full scale conquest, East Anglia fell, Northumbria and Mercia came under attack and the collectors of the Danegeld knocked at many a door. A new champion arose as Alfred held the Kingdom of Wessex and built the foundations for the recovery of lost territories.

OFFA'S DYKE

Some seventy miles of the dyke were constructed from about AD782 as Offa sought to lay down the marker of his extended territory. There are long continuous stretches and substantial gaps where the river did equal duty or boggy ground made incursions impractical to all but the foolhardy.

A similar construction more to the east known as Wats Dyke ran southward for thirty-eight miles from Holywell to a point below Oswestry. Both earthworks seem to be firmly set in the eighth century, Wats Dyke may belong to the reign of Ethelbald, but the similarity does not rule out the strong possibility that it too was the work of Offa's engineers.

Those parts of Offa's Dyke which are traversed by the ODP

include a good section from Sedbury Cliffs as far as Redbrook. It is rejoined above Kington en route for Knighton beyond which there is a particularly fine example as it rises to Llanfair Hill and onwards beyond Clun and over Edenhope Hill. It has a more modest profile as it crosses the fields to the east of Montgomery and briefly shadows a Roman road near Leighton. It is followed on the western side of Llanymynech Hill thus placing the fort in Mercian territory later passing through the woodland of Craig Forda to the west of Oswestry. The walker loses it finally as the Dee is approached beyond Chirk.

THE BORDER TODAY

In his *Description of Wales* written in AD1189 Giraldius recalls that once the Severn marked the boundary between the southern part of England and Wales and goes on to note that the Wye now marked the divide. Daniel Defoe, writing in about AD1725 referred to Herefordshire which lies to the west of the Severn, as once being part of Wales. Today only a mile of the Severn, below the confluence with the River Vyrnwy, serves as a boundary. The Wye performs this function from Redbrook to its meeting with the Severn below Chepstow and again, briefly, at Hay-on-Wye. Offa's Dyke shadows the modern boundary on its eastern side to Redbrook, is on the Welsh side as it approaches Knighton, beyond which it is firmly in Shropshire as it follows the high ground. It returns to Wales after crossing the Kerry Ridgeway and marks the division for two miles near Montgomery and again for three miles south of Chirk Castle. Thereafter the remaining sections are in Wales.

NOTE: As this book was being written the Government announced plans for the restructuring of local government in Wales. So far as the areas covered in this book are concerned it appears that in establishing single tier authorities Gwent and Clwyd may disappear and the old counties of Monmouthshire and Denbighshire "lost" after the 1974 reorganisation may return. Powys, covering the former counties of Radnorshire, Brecknockshire and Montgomery, seems set to remain.

2: The Lower Wye Valley
Sedbury Cliffs to Monmouth

MAPS: 1:25,000 Outdoor Leisure   14 Wye Valley & Forest of Dean
        1:50,000 Landranger   162 Gloucester & Forest of Dean

FACILITIES: Shops, refreshments and accommodation at Chepstow, Tintern & Monmouth. Inn at Brockweir. Refreshments and shop at Redbrook.

PARKING FOR ROUND WALKS: East of Offa's Dyke: Forestry Commission, Tiddenham Wood. West of the Wye: Chepstow Castle, Under Wyndcliff, Tintern Abbey, Tintern Old Station, Monmouth and "informal" near Bigsweir Bridge.

ALTERNATIVE ROUTES: From Madgett Hill, the Offa's Dyke Path splits giving a choice of a low level walk along the Wye or keeping to the higher ground via St Briavels Common. The two routes converge at Bigsweir Bridge. Neither of the Offa's Dyke paths visit Tintern Abbey, a diversion to Tintern is included in the text which reconnects to the ODP at Brockwier. All the routes have merit and are described in detail, and may be used in combination to provide round walks.

MILEAGE CHART:

Sedbury Cliffs to junction with recommended route from Chepstow	(1½)	
Chepstow Castle to Tintern turn		5
Tintern Abbey and on to rejoin the official route at Brockweir		2
Continuation of ODP to join lower route from Brockweir via Madgett Hill excluding Tintern	(1½)	
The route divides above Brockweir. Upper route via Hudnalls to Bigsweir Bridge	(2¾)	
Brockweir via river route to Bigsweir Bridge		3
Bigsweir Bridge to Lower Redbrook		3½
Redbrook to Wye Bridge Monmouth via The Kymin		3

Total for suggested route	16½
Total for official route	17¼

The first stage of the Offa's Dyke Path follows the lower Wye Valley on its eastern side as far as Monmouth with the upper route keeping to the dyke with some breaks as far as Redbrook. This is excellent walking country which is also blessed with another long distance path, The Wye Valley Walk, a 112 mile route from the mid-Wales town of Rhayader to Chepstow. Permutations of the Wye Valley Walk with the ODP provide easy to follow round walks with excursions into the nearby High Meadow area of the Forest of Dean.

From near Symonds Yat, upstream from Monmouth and not on our route, the Wye has cut a course which for much of the way runs under thickly wooded limestone cliffs of which Yat Rock is the best known but not necessarily the most exciting for the walker. This often dramatic terrain affords some spectacular views which continue south of Monmouth including on the ODP the sudden arrival at the top of a 200 feet cliff with a sheer fall to the Wye.

Peaceful as it is today the Forest of Dean, where coal and iron had been mined since before the Roman invasion, was once in equal competition with the iron masters of Kent and Sussex. An industry that extended into the Wye Valley with the charcoal burners playing an important part in providing fuel for the forges. Timber from the finest oaks in the forest was reserved for the Navy to build the "wooden walls of England"; the largest of the ships might require the felling of over 3,000 trees.

The port towns of the Wye were kept busy with an import/ export trade over many centuries, and ship building flourished along its banks. The river is tidal as far as Bigsweir, at Chepstow near its confluence with the Severn, the rise and fall is a remarkable 49 feet 6 inches. The river is famed for its salmon although apparently not so abundant as they once were. Gerald of Wales in his *Journey Through Wales* made in AD1188 mentions the large numbers of salmon and trout found in both the Wye and the Usk.

Another feature of the river scene, which may be witnessed in the Tintern area, is the arrival in early spring of huge numbers of elvers. They are completing a long journey from their birthplace in the Sargasso Sea to spend the next ten years growing to maturity in the rivers and streams further inland. These tiny creatures, no bigger than a thin finger, are in great demand to restock the rivers of Europe or as a delicacy - aphrodisiac qualities have been mentioned! The elvers are harvested with simple equipment, a large net, a bright light to which they are attracted and a bucket. In the season stretches of the Wye bank look as if they have just been invaded by a swarm of giant glow worms.

Offa had good reason for starting the construction of his dyke where he did but for the walker it is awkwardly located. The old joke about the Irishman who was asked for directions can be pressed into service, he replied "Well if I were you I wouldn't start from here". Many may find it more convenient to begin the day's walking from Chepstow although Sedbury Cliffs should not be dismissed out of hand if time allows, if only for the view offered to the Severn. The connection is made on the B4228 where it crosses the Sedbury/ Beachley road $^3/_4$ mile north of the Severn Bridge, from this point it is $^1/_4$ mile to the commemorative stone that marks the start.

SEDBURY CLIFFS TO THE JUNCTION WITH THE ROUTE FROM CHEPSTOW

The ODP starts from a spot where the watery vice of Wye and Severn have squeezed the land into a narrowing peninsular. A block of rough stone is set on the Dyke above the cliffs. It bears the simple inscription in Welsh and English, "Llwybr Clawdd Offa, Offa's Dyke Path - This marks the start and finish of a 168 mile long distance footpath designated by the Countryside Commission". A place where old and new almost meet. Pause for a moment and look over the gorse to the Severn, Britain's longest river. Upstream there are places where the river is more than 2 miles wide but between Aust Rock and Beachley Point it narrows to provide an ancient crossing of the river used from at least Roman times. Now the 400 feet high towers and a webb of steel wires that suspend the Severn and Wye Bridge stand silhouetted against the sky. The centre span of the bridge, opened in 1966, is 3,240 feet in length with side spans of 1,000 feet each. From here the great juggernauts move amongst the threads reduced to the size of a child's plaything, their thunder lost on the air. Immediately below the cliff waders paddle the sandbanks and you may get a glimpse of the sharp outline of that ever patient fisherman, a heron standing stock still waiting for the moment to strike. In front of you a long fence only fully visible at low tide projects into the water. This is a putcheon weir, another can be observed from the public footpath on the Severn Bridge. The weir, a device that has been in use in the tidal reaches of the river for hundreds of years is a static, and you may think barbaric, method of catching salmon. In season hundreds of cone-like basketwork traps (metal framing is now more frequently used) six feet or so in length are fixed into the structure four, five or six "stories" high. The salmon, trapped head first in the narrowing basket, cannot escape and are collected as the tide ebbs.

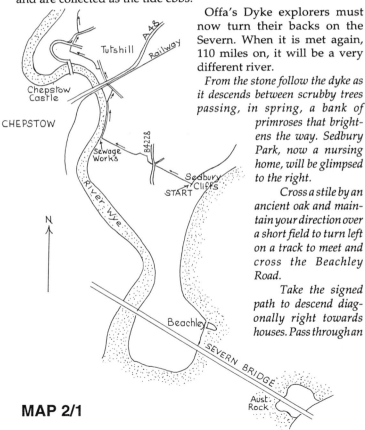

Offa's Dyke explorers must now turn their backs on the Severn. When it is met again, 110 miles on, it will be a very different river.

From the stone follow the dyke as it descends between scrubby trees passing, in spring, a bank of primroses that brightens the way. Sedbury Park, now a nursing home, will be glimpsed to the right.

Cross a stile by an ancient oak and maintain your direction over a short field to turn left on a track to meet and cross the Beachley Road.

Take the signed path to descend diagonally right towards houses. Pass through an

MAP 2/1

ungated gap in a hedge and over a bank (apparently a disused railway), to cross a lane and stream to reach a housing estate, initially with some aptly named streets until inspiration ran out.

Take the road ahead and in 40 yards turn left on the path found opposite Norse Way. A rather urban progress so quickly reached after the wilds of the Severn and fortunately not the herald of what is to come. In 100 yards turn right on Mercian Way. Continue beyond the road junction by Offa's Close; the houses are left behind as the road narrows to a track with the white limestone cliffs seen in contrast to the green meadows below.

The track falls to pass Sedbury Sewage Treatment Works. As the track bends left take the path on the right, over a stile and pursuing it with garden fences on your right and a stable to your left. A further stile is crossed with the Wye seen immediately below to the left, a row of bungalows to your right and glimpses forward to Chepstow Castle. The path soon meets a road but keep close to the fence on your left, passing Wye Bank Place, and briefly between a hedge and houses.

On rejoining the road turn left through a bungalow estate, following Wyebank Avenue. Turn right at Wyebank Drive to meet a main road, where turn left soon crossing the railway and the Chepstow bypass. In about 250 yards take the signed tarmac path on the left which provides a good view to Chepstow Castle, the Wye and John Rastrick's delicately arched iron bridge of 1816.

As you meet a white house veer left to follow a narrow way hemmed in by a high wall and an ivy bank. The descending path brings a briefly improved view to Chepstow before climbing steeply to meet a lane. Here bear left on a path running between almost fortress-like walls descending to meet the junction with the route from Chepstow. Turn right here, details follow after information on Chepstow.

CHEPSTOW

Chepstow is the first port town of the Wye with a long history of ship building and import/export trading. Wine was shipped in from France from early times and later locally quarried stone was sent by boat down the Severn estuary to Portishead and to construct Newport docks. Daniel Defoe, reporting during his *Tour of the Whole of Britain* (1724-27), painted a picture of a flourishing town and referred to the large quantities of wheat exported from Chepstow. There was a glass factory in the town during the eighteenth century,

Chepstow Castle

a tradition that continues today with Stuart Crystal. The plentiful supply of timber which encouraged the ship builders also supplied the raw materials for the large scale production of bobbins for the Yorkshire weaving industry from about 1860.

It is the castle that will attract the visitor's immediate attention, reputed to be the first to be built in stone in this country. Standing on a sheer cliff it dominates both the town and river, a picture of medieval strength that was to persist until the siege cannon brought about a change in military tactics. The castle was built by William Fitz Osbern, a great supporter of William the Conqueror. He actively encouraged William in his plans to invade Britain, providing a large number of ships. Following the victory at Hastings, Fitz Osbern was created Earl of Hereford charged with the protection of the border between England and South Wales. Military Governor might conceivably have been a better title for he was in almost continuous conflict with the Welsh. Fitz Osbern also built other Wye-side castles at Monmouth, Hereford and Clifford.

Chepstow Castle was considerably enlarged in the following

centuries as the Normans tightened their hold on Britain. The Civil War which broke out in 1642 was to bring an end to its military value. It was held for the Royalist cause by the Earl of Worcester until 1645 when it succumbed to the Parliamentary army, after a heavy bombardment. The Royalists were again garrisoning the castle when hostilities reopened in 1646 but once again it fell to Cromwell's forces. The man in command at that time was Sir Nicholas Kemeys, the county's Member of Parliament and High Sheriff of Glamorgan and Monmouth. He died, not during the attack, but was executed after the castle's surrender.

Sir Henry Winter (or Wintour), with 300 of his men, was briefly Governor of Chepstow Castle in 1645, but his story will be told as the walk progresses upstream.

Following the restoration of the monarchy in 1660 Henry Marten was imprisoned here for twenty years; his enforced but not uncomfortable lodgings, although built much earlier, still retain the name Marten's Tower. Henry Marten's signature appears with fifty-eight others on the death warrant of Charles I drawn at the High Court of Justice on 29 January 1648. Little did he know that the signature which condemned the king to public execution in Whitehall was to serve as his own indictment.

Whatever the rights and wrongs that led to the Civil War, Martens story is far from attractive. He was a Grays Inn lawyer who married for money, an unhappy loveless union. By 1640 he was engaged in politics as one of the members for Berkshire. He seems to have been a womaniser with an unsavoury reputation. Charles I reportedly put it in stronger terms when he is said to have described him as an ugly rascal and a whore master.

Marten made no secret of his vindictive opposition to the monarchy. He was one of the members of the Committee of Safety which recommended the raising of an army to resist the alleged intentions of the king to bring military power to bear upon Parliament. Shortly before war broke out Charles was seeking Marten's trial on charges of high treason.

Marten, who was made governor of Reading, donated a large sum of money to the Parliamentary cause and promised to provide a cavalry regiment. In 1643 as a result of his support for the removal of the monarchy he was deprived of his seat in the Commons and briefly confined in the Tower of London. Later he was governor of Aylesbury and took part in the siege of Dennington Castle.

Whilst held prisoner at Chepstow he composed his own epitaph in the form of an acrostic - the initial letter of each line spelling out his name thus:

> Here or elsewhere (all's one to you or me)
> Earth, air or water gripes my ghostless duty
> None knows how soon to be my fire set free
> Reader, if you an oft tried rule will trust
> You'll gladly do and suffer what you must
> My life was spent in serving yours and you
> And death's my pay (it seems) and welcome too
> Revenge destroying but itself, while I
> To birds of prey leave my cage and fly.
> Examples preach to the eye. Care then (mine says)
> Not how you end, but how you spend your days.

The town's fine parish church, St Mary's has its origin in a Benedictine monastery founded in 1072. Among its interesting monuments is the colourful tomb of Henry Somerset, 2nd Earl of Worcester, Lord Herbert of Chepstow, Raglan and Gower, he and his wife lie here in some splendour attired in coronation robes. A rather grim Father Time with hour glass and scythe looks over the tomb of Thomas Shipman and his wife with their twelve children praying before them.

Chepstow was a popular port of call for those taking the Wye Tour during the late eighteenth and early nineteenth centuries. A selection of their work inspired by the journey down the river, prose, poetry and prints can be seen in the museum close to the castle. Many other aspects of the town's history are featured including an exhibition of salmon and eel fishing.

It was from the quay at Chepstow, close to the Willow Tree Restaurant, that the leaders of the Chartist March on Newport in 1839, John Frost a former mayor, William Jones and Sarfarnie Williams, were transported to Tasmania. They had been arraigned at Monmouth Assizes charged with treason, found guilty and condemned to death, later commuted to a long exile.

CHEPSTOW TO THE TINTERN DIVERSION

From the castle car park turn left into Bridge Street, soon passing the 300-year-old Bridge Inn.

The inn was originally called, appropriately enough, The Ship and Castle, but changed its name to commemorate the construction of Rastrick's iron bridge of 1816 a five arched spanning of the river supported on tall stone columns. The huge tidal rise of over 49 feet robs the river of some of its appeal; gone are the clear waters to be enjoyed further upstream, instead the water swirls opaquely in milk chocolate brown eddies. George Borrow on the last night of a long tour records in his *Wild Wales* that having sampled the water at the sources of both Severn and Wye he ventured down to the riverside to retaste the water. One can only conclude it must have been a very dark night! From the centre of the bridge where the boundary between Wales and England is picked out in letters of white and gold, there is a fine view to the castle.

Once over the bridge take the footpath opposite (next to Wye Cliff House) which climbs between walls to be joined from the right by the Sedbury section of the ODP. Maintain your direction between ivy covered walls to a

MAP 2/2

N

TINTERN ABBEY

Devil's Pulpit

Cliffs

Quarry

Dennelhill Farm

RIVER WYE

B4228

Wallhope Grove

Wintour's Leap

Lancaut Nature Reserve

Tower

Mopla Road

CHEPSTOW CASTLE

short flight of steps to meet and cross the main road. Go forward on a minor road (Mopla Road) and follow this for about 200 yards to turn left on a path which climbs gently through a field of buttercups and daisies. In a field behind the white bungalow there is an old lookout tower, its original purpose now obscure.

At the end of the field the path is funnelled towards an iron gate, here turn right over a stile and on through a field with a wall on your left. At the end of the wall turn left over a stile, soon bearing right on a metalled track.

In a short distance turn left over a stile crossing a field towards woodland. On meeting a stile take care not to go ahead on the attractive path that leads through the Lancaut Nature reserve but turn right to reach the B4228 in 200 yards and turn left.

In 100 yards turn left under a stone arch bearing the legend Moyle Old School Lane to follow a climbing path leading to a pair of kissing gates. Continue to cross a metalled lane with the narrow path between houses and a hedge allowing occasional glimpses down to the Wye.

Soon a diversion of a few steps will bring you out to a high unfenced rocky cliff with a dizzying drop and a welcome view to the wider world.

BROAD ROCK AND WINTOUR'S LEAP

Here, for those not over bothered by heights there is a fine unfettered bird's-eye view over the green canopy of the trees, almost Amazonian in character. A prospect that is likely to be shared with a great flock of vociferous jackdaws who make their home in these high rock towers.

More distantly buzzards soar over the trees that sweep down to the banks of the Wye. These birds, so graceful in their easy flight, are seen throughout the long course of the river; I have noted as many as eight high in the summer sky above Tintern Abbey. If you should be here in the early days of spring you may see their twirling courtship display. This is the site of one of the great escapes and you will shortly be asked to suspend your incredulity as the story of Sir John Wintour unfolds, but first the view that is hidden from the motorist although the road is only a few steps away.

Beyond our own eyrie is the green topped cliff of Broad Rock with two or three magnificently situated houses. Below, the river coils snake-like under the cliffs in one of its great meandering loops almost enclosing the farms and pastures of Lancaut. High above the northern curve of the river a white limestone face breaks through the green curtain of the tree-covered Wyndcliff. Here from the Eagles Nest reached by the "365 steps" is another great viewpoint with a vista that extends far beyond the Wye to encompass the wider territory of the Severn.

Below us lies the Lancaut Nature Reserve, a jumble of rocks from earlier quarrying and a straightish stretch of the Wye. On this reach you may see diminutive water skiers skimming like waterboatmen but with rather more disturbance. If your timing is impeccable, or by extraordinary chance, you may look down on the desperate last hour of the three day, 100 mile raft race which starts from Hay-on-Wye, a gruelling challenge held over the Spring Bank Holiday weekend.

Sir John Wintour (otherwise Winter) was a man of great wealth, an ironmaster and forester with a forge at Lydney and a lessee from the crown of a large acreage of the Forest of Dean. Sir John was an ardent Royalist, supporting Charles I regardless of the cost to purse or person. As a local commander during the Civil War he made himself a considerable nuisance to the Parliamentarians based in Gloucester and the surrounding countryside. On one occasion, after a skirmish at Tiddenham, he was hotly pursued by the enemy, only evading capture by scrambling down the 200 feet cliff to the river. A story like this loses nothing in the telling and was embellished to suggest that Sir John galloped his horse over the edge...and survived. Thus we have Wintour's Leap.

Rather better attested is the scorched earth policy he was obliged to adopt. By 1645 Sir Edward Massey, the commander of the Gloucester forces was having increasing success against Wintour's troops. Fearful that his house and more importantly his ironworks should fall into their hands Wintour destroyed both and took refuge in Chepstow. After exile he returned to the Forest of Dean upon the restoration of the monarchy to pick up the tattered threads of his former industry.

Clearly Wintour was a man of resource, it is interesting to note that he experimented with a process to turn coal to coke some years before the birth of Abraham Darby. It was he, it will be remembered, who in the next century after much patient research evolved the smelting of iron from coke and set the wheels of the Industrial Revolution in motion.

THE WALK CONTINUED

A few steps will bring you to the road. B4228, turn left to follow it for just over ¹/₄ mile, a sudden switch from the spectacular to the mundane.

Shortly after passing Netherhope Lane, turn right over a stone stile to cross a field, possibly occupied by Jacobs sheep with their brown patched white fleeces and horns to add a touch of dignity. Continue into Wallhope Grove where the path soon swings to the left. Beyond the wood field paths, from which there is a retrospective view to the Severn Bridge, lead back to the road.

Turn right on the road (B4228 again!) and in ¹/₂ mile, turn left on the path found just short of Dennelhill Farm. The fenced path runs under trees to reach a stile and an English Heritage notice which announces "Offa's Dyke Tidenham section". A few steps forward allows a downward view to the Tintern Quarry where limestone and granite are still hewn from the hillside.

The line of the dyke is now followed to the Tintern diversion. There are twists and turns, dips and rises but keep to the crest of the cliff as you make your way through the woods for 1¹/₄ miles to the Devil's Pulpit via the Boatwood Plantation and Worgans Wood, crossing two forest roads en route. Any uncertainties resolved by waymarking on rocks and trees.

The Wye, far below, is largely hidden by the trees and an often hazy atmosphere serves to create an impression that the traveller is peering down to a deeply distant blue sea. Views are in short supply, grudgingly granted at intervals, but all the more valued when offered. The walker who travels with a camera must take his chance when he can and not hold back in the hope of something better. The best opportunities are found along Plumweir Cliff. Shut in, may be, but not lacking in interest, the woods are full of bird song, a startled buzzard may take noisy flight, woodpeckers drill away at the trees and a number of badger setts will be noted at intervals to Madgett Hill.

The dyke makes a sharp turn as Plumweir Cliff is reached. In a short distance there is a classic view from a little rocky platform that opens a window in the woodland. What a view it is, a narrow angle squint through the branches up the Wye Valley to Tintern Abbey, a secret view to a stone

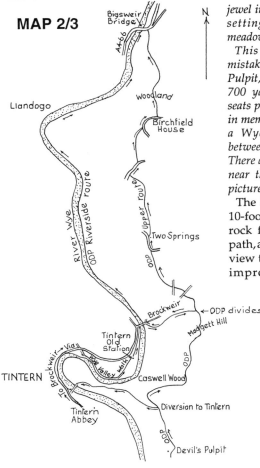

MAP 2/3

jewel in the emerald green setting of the water meadows.

This should not be mistaken for the Devil's Pulpit, which is reached in 700 yards, after passing seats placed along the way in memory of Chris Pugh, a Wye Valley Warden between 1972 and 1983. There are more open views near the seats and better picture opportunities.

The Devil's Pulpit is a 10-foot high column of rock found just off the path, again with a distant view to the Abbey, now improved by recent trimming of the trees. It was from here that he is traditionally said to have preached to the monks in an attempt to divert them from their calling.

Continue with the ODP, soon directed left signed Monmouth with a descent by a stepped path and more badger setts to be seen in the banks. About 600 yards from the Devil's Pulpit the path divides. The ODP continues northward but a visit to Tintern is suggested, beyond which the official route may be joined at Brockweir. The description of the high level route follows the Tintern diversion.

31

Tintern Abbey and the Wye Valley from the ODP

OPTION A
DIVERSION TO TINTERN - ONE MILE

From the junction take the falling path signed off left. The route is well waymarked. On meeting a wider path turn right and in a few yards left, soon making a steep rocky descent to a T-junction of paths where turn right. The path falls to meet the track of the former Wye Valley Railway, where turn right and then swing left soon to cross the bridge over the Wye to reach Tintern. Turn left along the road passing Abbey Mill to reach Tintern Abbey.

TINTERN

The Cistercian foundation dates from 1131 when the then Lord of Chepstow, Walter Fitz Richard, encouraged a band of monks to settle here in this peaceful spot by the river. The fishing, an important consideration to those following a strict regime, was excellent, and

The Wye Bridge, Chepstow
The Tower, The Kymin, Monmouth, Gwent

The Black Mountains - the Hatterall ridge from
Pentwyn hill fort, Gwent
St Mary's Church, Capel y ffin

stone and timber were easily available for building. The monastery did well, aided by generous grants of land. Little of the original building remains but the foundations of extensions in the following century give a clear indication of its growth. Only the abbey church stands today, albeit roofless. From within, the 270 feet long nave's high arched windows frame views to the hills. Around the church lie the low walls of the many domestic buildings, dormitories, kitchens, dining hall and infirmary.

The monks, or more probably the lay brothers, were involved in the iron industry, said to have been introduced by the Cistercians, although iron and coal had been mined in the Forest of Dean for many centuries before the Romans arrived to exploit its mineral resources. The plentiful supply of charcoal kept the forges glowing long after the dissolution of the monastery in 1538. An easily missed plaque on a wall by the abbey marks the spot where thirty years later brass was first made by alloying copper with zinc.

Almost inevitably the Abbey fell into ruin, its stone a ready-made quarry for builders, its leaded roof equally valuable. Covered in ivy it was to prove a romantic magnet for the Wye Valley explorers of the eighteenth and nineteenth centuries. John Byng, author of the Torrington Diaries, had his own special recipe: he recommended that to enjoy the abbey to the full a table within the nave should be spread with a sumptous picnic to the accompaniment of the music of a Welsh harpist. It conjures up a pretty picture but not one that might easily win the approval of its present guardians, Welsh Historic Monuments.

THE WALK CONTINUED TO BROCKWEIR

The ODP can be rejoined at Brockweir by retracing your steps over the Wye and taking a signed and waymarked low level path from Tintern but an alternative via a short riverside section of the Wye Valley Walk is suggested.

Take the road, the A466, back through the village to join the Wye Valley Walk by St Michaels church. The path runs through the churchyard before following the Wye upstream for 700 yards to reach and climb the embankment of the former railway. Turn left following the track to reach Tintern Old Station.

The station has been restored to its Victorian origins with an exhibition centre in an old railway coach in the livery of the Great Western Railway, recounting the history of the single track line between Monmouth and Chepstow which opened in 1876. Initially designed for commercial traffic it later carried passengers on what must have been a highly scenic route. There is a picnic site, car parking throughout the year and refreshments during the summer months. A poster of 1890 solicits passengers for an excursion to the Military Exhibition being staged at the Royal Hospital, Chelsea.

From the station continue northwards along the track passing through a belt of woodland to mount steps to cross Brockweir Bridge.

OPTION B

CONTINUATION FROM DEVIL'S PULPIT TO BROCKWEIR VIA MADGETT HILL

From the Devil's Pulpit continue your northward progress along the dyke, soon turning left on a descending path. When the sign to Tintern is reached remain with the ODP, now signed Brockweir 1½ miles. After a dark passage through Caswell Wood daylight is seen ahead and the first distant glimpse of Brockweir.

The path descends along the inside edge of the wood to meet a crossing path by a wooden barrier. Maintain your direction falling gently through the woodland; this is the start of a long and quite superb descent to Brockweir with fine views unfolded as progress is made.

The wood is left by a stile and a further English Heritage notice and now terraces Madgett Hill as the land falls sharply away to your left with only a veiled view permitted by a thin ribbon of trees. In about 200 yards a waymarked ash tree and marker post direct you left making a stepped descent into an open field.

Here there is a good prospect down to Brockweir with its white and colourwashed houses and the thin white lines of the Wye bridge. Beyond the river are the forested hills through which the Wye Valley Walk threads its way. Directly ahead beyond the valley lies the high ground of St Briavels Common with a scatter of houses and farms set amid a network of small fields, a preview of the upper Offa's Dyke Path.

Descend to the opposite fence line where bear right and in 60 yards turn left over a stile briefly following a hedged path. In a short distance, just below a semi-derelict barn there is a further parting of the ways as the upper route via St Briavels Common and Hudnalls is marked by a large double signpost. This route, option D, will be described after the lower level route; the two converge at Bigsweir Bridge.

For Brockweir bear half left following the hedgeline as you continue your descent through pasture. At the foot of the hill pass the stables of the Horse and Pony Protection Association on your right. You will have already seen some of their clients, Thelwall like Shetland ponies with manes hanging over their eyes amongst them.

Turn right passing the sign to the Moravian church and the Malt House to reach the road by the Brockweir Country Inn with its handsome sign showing a badger against the easily recognised local landscape. There is a badger weather vane in the garden of one of the riverside houses by the bridge.

BROCKWEIR

Pretty little Brockweir, set on the river bank under the tree crowned hills, a comfortable huddle of houses and the whitewashed Moravian

Pretty little Brockweir - once a river port of the Wye

church with its tall lancet windows facing on to the Wye, as pleasant a place as any along the river. It lies a mile or two below the normal tidal limit and served as a transhipment port with goods destined for towns further upstream being moved into shallower draught vessels hauled by men or horses. It was a work-a-day place peopled by ship builders, waggoners, traders and sailors awaiting the turn of the tide or a fresh cargo. No church, but not lacking in cider houses where hard earned money was easily spent, the liquid fuel of rowdiness and disorder. The village's unenviable reputation led to the establishment of the Moravian church in 1833. If you missed visiting it on your way through the village you can see it from the bridge.

OPTION C
THE WYESIDE ROUTE

Having crossed the bridge from the Tintern Abbey route, turn immediately left along the Quayside, signed Bigsweir 3 miles, keeping to the riverside. An easy route to follow needing little in the way of detailed directions. 2 miles upstream the village of Llandogo is seen on the far bank with houses dotted up the hillside. The path widens to a track which is followed under trees. When Bigsweir House is approached leave the wide track and follow the waymarked path on the left that passes through a conservation area. Leave the river at Bigsweir Bridge, built in 1829 as part of the St Arvans-Redbrook Turnpike over the river, the inevitable toll house will be seen on the west side. Bigsweir also marks the normal tidal limit of the Wye.

Here the route which kept to the high ground of St Briavels Common merges and the ODP continues without further division or diversion to Monmouth.

OPTION D
MADGETT HILL TO BIGSWEIR VIA ST BRIAVELS COMMON

As previously mentioned the ODP splits on the lower slopes of Madgett Hill. The upper way provides an enjoyable crossing of St Briavels Common by a succession of tiny lanes and old tracks that you could well imagine being used by strings of packhorses or drovers. Some of the tracks are rather too narrow for large scale droving which needed a width of about 40 feet, but later in the walk a classic drove road will be followed over the hills on the way to Kington.

St Briavels, which lies off our route, was once the "capital" of the Forest of Dean. The Domesday Book records that prior to the conquest the Lords of the Manor of Little Dean and Micheldean held their land free of tax in return for overseeing the forest. The Normans greatly valued Dean for its hunting and made it a Royal Forest protected by harsh laws, with only the King allowed to hunt the deer and wild boar. The forest was administered from St Briavels where the Constable of the Castle was also the Lord Warden of the Forest, holding his office under the king. He was assisted in his duties by lesser officials like the agisters who were responsible for collecting rents from those who grazed their sheep or whose pigs fed off the acorns and beech mast. The strangely named Keeper of the Gawle saw to the collection of the royalties of those licensed to mine coal and iron. The Foresters of Fee were entrusted with the care of the "vert and venison". Venison is clear enough but vert referred to all that bore green leaves in the forest and the rights of cutting. Their payment was in kind, with grazing and pannage free of charge and the ownership of storm felled trees. Today the castle gatehouse is a youth hostel with a certain cachet, after all King John slept there!

From the signposted division of paths head northwards, down a steep bank to meet and cross a tumbling stream, then climbing through a short belt of sheltered woodland to meet a minor road. Turn right and almost immediately left. The track curves to the right but go ahead between hedges with banks of snowdrops to be seen in season.

The way dips to cross a bridge over a small stream soon to reach a narrow lane. Turn left then almost immediately right on a hedged track, crossing yet another stream and continuing on a gently rising hollow lane. Cross another lane by a house called Shangri La and maintain your direction on a narrow hedged path, stony under foot, with occasional views to the west through the broken hedgerow.

Turn left on meeting another lane, then bearing right, still climbing and passing an Edward VII letter box set in the wall by a house called Fernleigh.

When you reach the house called Two Springs leave the main lane bearing right on a narrower track which rises past a house to your left clearly converted from the chapel that once served the small community.

The ODP continues to climb steadily between walls, intermittently rocky under foot. In about 600 yards turn left at a T-junction of paths. In 200 yards turn left on a wider track and about 40 yards before a white house is reached bear right to cross a short field to reach a stile set in a stone wall by a tall beech tree. Descend to a lane passing barns to your right. Turn right to follow the lane for 200 yards passing Denehurst.

Take the wide track on the left signed Bigsweir 1¹/₄ miles which narrows to meet a broader track where bear right passing a white house to your left beyond which turn right on a wide track. In 100 yards turn left at a T-junction, descending between old walls to a further junction and turn right. In 200 yards, just before a large white house, Birchfield, turn left descending steeply on a walled path into woodland to meet a crossing path. Here turn right and in 40 paces left, with an initial steep descent aided by a short flight of steps which bridges an awkward section.

From here follow a clear gently winding track, near the bottom edge of the wood bear right to meet a stile and emerge into an open field with a view down to Bigsweir Bridge.

Head directly over the field towards a long line of ancient sweet chestnuts. One is hollowed out like a sentry box and you may wonder what miracle of nature continues to keep it upright. Sweet chestnuts are common in this part of the country. They were introduced by the Romans and later one tree in ten that was planted in the Forest of Dean was a sweet chestnut.

Beyond the trees cross a stile and descend diagonally left in the direction of Bigsweir Bridge. At the bottom of the field turn right on a wide track which leads to the road, the A466, both branches of the ODP now reunited.

BIGSWEIR TO MONMOUTH VIA REDBROOK AND THE KYMIN

At Bigsweir turn right on the A466 and in a few yards right again on minor road signed St Briavels, Coleford and Welcome to Gloucestershire.

Keep with the road for 700 yards, after passing a path signed off to St Briavels Youth Hostel on your right, turn left on a tarmac driveway and in about 200 yards enter woodland, mostly beech and oak. From here to Redbrook there are stretches of Offa's Dyke, the last to be seen until after

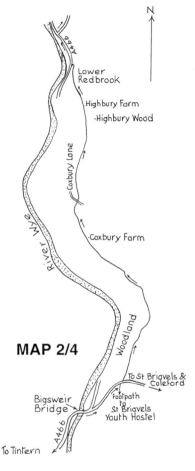

N

Lower
Redbrook

Highbury Farm
·Highbury Wood

Coxbury Lane

River Wye

·Coxbury Farm

Woodland

MAP 2/4

To St Briavels &
Coleford

Bigsweir
Bridge

Footpath
to
St Briavels
Youth Hostel

A466

To Tintern

Kington.

Follow the clear path roughly northwards for well over ½ mile. Beyond the wood continue through fields with the woodland to your left for ½ mile to enter the wood once more. In a few yards bear half right briefly following the inside edge of the wood, then over a field passing Coxbury Farm on your right, with views to the Wye.

Beyond the farm maintain your forward direction over fields with the boundary to the right to pass through a short stretch of woodland. Cross a stile a little before the end of the field and bear diagonally right climbing through trees to reach and cross Coxbury Lane.

A stile leads into the broadleafed woodland of Highbury Wood Nature Reserve to take a rising path which bears left at a mound. Follow the dyke northwards through the wood for ¾ mile to Highbury Farm.

Beyond a stile turn immediately left on a falling track passing a wireless mast. In 100 yards bear left to cross a stile and over a short field to a further stile seen in the direction of the former railway bridge now only used by travellers on the Wye Valley Walk. There is a fine view characteristic of the lower valley of the Wye with the river flowing beneath wooded hills.

The path makes a steep descent towards houses to reach a lane. Turn right and just beyond a junction turn left descending steps past the back

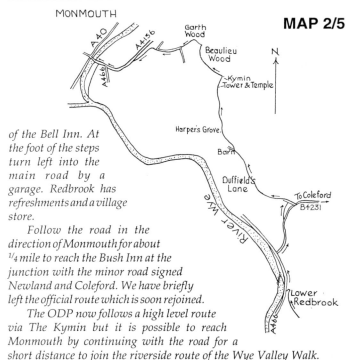

MAP 2/5

of the Bell Inn. At the foot of the steps turn left into the main road by a garage. Redbrook has refreshments and a village store.

Follow the road in the direction of Monmouth for about ¼ mile to reach the Bush Inn at the junction with the minor road signed Newland and Coleford. We have briefly left the official route which is soon rejoined.

The ODP now follows a high level route via The Kymin but it is possible to reach Monmouth by continuing with the road for a short distance to join the riverside route of the Wye Valley Walk.

From the Bush Inn follow the Newland Road for 700 yards to take the signed path on the left which climbs to Duffield's Lane, to reach the open hillside with excellent views. About ½ mile after passing Duffield Farm a stone barn is reached on your left. (Note this may now have been converted to residential use).

At this point leave the track by a stile on the right. Turn immediately left and maintain your direction northwards through fields and a fenced path which emerges into the National Trust's Kymin property.

THE KYMIN

"Tis distance lends enchantment to the view" wrote Thomas Campbell, the Scottish poet. It was an idea that clearly coloured the thinking of a group of the leading gentlemen of Monmouth in the late eighteenth century. They were well placed both financially and geographically to put the concept into practice when they sought a suitable site to establish a place of relaxation well away from their everyday responsibilities.

They did not have far to look, for the place of their dreams was staring them in the face every time they lifted their eyes above street level. Just one mile outside the busy town the 800 feet tree topped Kymin rose quickly to give a commanding view. Here they laid out a bowling green and built a dining club, a round turreted observation tower.

A year of two later, in 1800, they built a commemorative temple to "perpetuate the names of those Noble Admirals who distinguished themselves by their glorious victories for England in the last and present wars". Distinguished service and glorious victories indeed with no less than sixteen admirals named on plaques that carry dates ranging from 1759 to 1801. Crowning the temple is the figure of Britannia and to quote the inscription "...seated on a rock, the painting in front represents the standards of Great Britain waving triumphant over the fallen and captive flags of France, Spain and Holland".

The full list of plaques is: 1759 Hawke, 1793 Gell (one of his noteworthy exploits was the capture of a Spanish ship carrying treasure of enormous worth), 1793 Hood, 1794 Howe, 1795 Cornwallis, 1795 Bridport, 1797 Duncan, 1798 Rodney, 1798 Warren, 1799 Keith, 1799 Mitchell, 1801 Parker, 1797 Vincent, 1798 Nelson, 1759 Boscawen and 1797 Thomson.

Heroes in their day but not all so well known now. Space does not allow the telling of all their stories but a brief reference is made to some of those honoured here. Edward, Lord Hawke, Admiral of the Fleet joined the navy, like so many others, at the tender age of fourteen. In 1759 he was in command of a fleet when an invasion of England was feared. His task was to keep the French from putting to sea which he achieved by one of the longest and most difficult blockades confining the enemy fleet to harbour at Brest from May to November.

Howe left Eton to join the navy one year earlier than even Hawke. The culmination of his long career was the "Glorious first of June", 1794, in command of the fleet that defeated the French off Ushant.

Hood's special mention seems to refer to his capture of Toulon, and Boscawen. He was known as "Old Dreadnought" after one of his earlier commands, for his victory over the French at Lagos Bay.

Nelson whose victory and death at Trafalgar took place five years after the opening of the temple is honoured for his decisive victory at the Battle of the Nile in 1798.

Today the National Trust is the guardian of both tower and restored temple. The view is as fine as ever, looking down to Monmouth with the busy traffic now reduced to toy-like proportions, more agreeably the river and mile upon mile of rolling countryside with the Sugar Loaf in the far distance.

THE ROUTE TO MONMOUTH

From the tower head north for 50 yards then bear left signed Monmouth 1 mile, to make the long descent of the hill. First on a rocky stepped path through woodland where in spring wood anemones are succeeded by the ubiquitous bluebell. After 100 yards or so turn right and continue downhill with a fence to your left to meet a metalled lane.

Turn right and in a few yards cross a stile found on the right to reach and enter Garth Wood in 300 yards. The descent is continued with the path swinging west to reach a lane (Kymin Road).

Follow the lane for 300 yards and as it bends to the right leave it to join a track by a metal gate. Another wooded section is soon reached beyond a kissing gate from where a path leads down to the A4136 and on to the junction with the A466.

Ignore the turn to Tintern and continue to cross the Wye Bridge to reach Monmouth at the busy A40.

3: Monmouth to Pandy

MAPS: 1:25,000 Pathfinder   1087 (SO 41/51)
          1086 (SO 21/31)   1063 (SO 22/32) (small section)
          1:50,000 Landranger   162 Gloucester & Forest of Dean
                                        (small section at Monmouth end)
          161 Abergavenny & Black Mountains

FACILITIES: Shops, refreshments and accommodation in Monmouth,
    several B&B at inns or houses en route including Pandy and bunkhouse
    at Llangattock Lingoed.

MILEAGE CHART:

Wye Bridge Monmouth to Llanfihangel Ystum Llywern	6½
Llantilio Crossenny	3
White Castle	2
Llangattock Lingoed	3
Pandy	2¼
Total	16¾

This section follows the official route throughout.

From Monmouth the ODP crosses a different but appealing countryside. Gone are the great waters of the Wye, instead its tributaries, the Monnow and Trothy, and lesser streams, some so small that they merit only the thinest of blue veins upon the map. This is mainly sheep country, for many centuries <u>the</u> great wealth of Britain. In Herefordshire they spoke of the Leominster Ore, not the hard yellow glint of gold but soft fleecy riches shorn from the millions of sheep that grazed the hills.

The ODP to Pandy is an excellent forerunner to the crossing of the Black Mountains, perhaps enjoyed to the full during the lambing season. The way winds through a gently rolling landscape with the occasional steeper ascent of brief duration, but with its modest heights providing some very fine views. Field paths over short cropped grass meet quiet lanes leading to long settled villages. Here in the villages and at the White Castle may be seen some of the colourful, sometimes bloodstained, threads of a rich historical tapestry.

MONMOUTH

The signs at the entrance to the town announce "Monmouth ancient border town" they speak nothing but the truth but even Monmouth is discovering that it may be older than it suspected. The River Monnow throws a protective curving arm around the western edge of the town, the Wye is at its eastern door. Both have been bridged for at least 800 years. Today's, still narrow, many arched stone bridge over the Wye, is a successor to one known to have been here in the thirteenth century. The present Monnow Bridge dates from about 1270 but during work to improve the town's flood defences in 1988 the timbers of an earlier bridge were uncovered which have been dated 130 years earlier. The bridge has a unique feature, a 700-year old fortified gatehouse, the only one remaining in Britain, and still something of a hindrance to traffic!

The street plan has changed little from the early development of the town, an asset to the archaeologists who have been digging deep into Monmouth's past in Monnow Street. Here a vacant shop provided the opportunity for a careful unveiling of the past, the initial intention to trace the town walls. The removal of silt and sand deposited during flooding has uncovered the remains of a fourteenth-century house. Slag from forges of the thirteenth and fourteenth centuries confirms the town's long association with the iron industry.

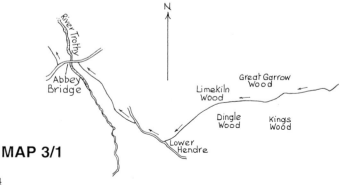

MAP 3/1

Butcher's pole axes show a change of use to a slaughter house. Amongst other discoveries was a medieval silver penny. Digging deeper a pre-Norman house has been discovered and now Roman remains are appearing as brush and trowel gently sift through the debris of the ages.

The Romans, quick to recognise a strategically important site when they saw one, established a station here, Blestium, and were involved in iron founding by the Monnow.

William Fitz Osbern built the first castle in 1068 which was extended and strengthened in the following century. It was here in 1387 that the future Henry V, victor of Agincourt, was born. The battle on St Crispins Day, 1415, during the Hundred Years War, was a remarkable triumph when the king's heavily outnumbered army inflicted a crushing defeat on the French, a victory in which the Welsh archers played a decisive role. Henry was a seasoned warrior; when only seventeen he was in charge of the English forces trying to stem the tide of Welsh raids under Owain Glyndwr which ravished the countryside of Herefordshire and Monmouthshire. Although the Welsh did not succeed in breaking through the town's defences the havoc created in the area had a serious effect on the local economy over a period of years.

The castle was reduced after the Civil War; in 1673 the Marquess of Worcester built a handsome residence on the site, Great Castle House. It now houses the regimental museum of the Royal Monmouthshire Royal Engineers (Militia), justly proud of the honour of being the first regiment of the reserve British army. The museum tells not only the story of the regiment but something of the town's military history. There is a collection of rifles from the Brown Bess,

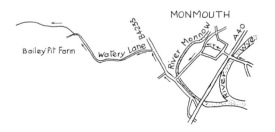

45

via the Lee Enfield to the Kalashnicov. Wandering round the museum an interesting comparison can be made with the inaccurate Brown Bess, in use with the army for 100 years and the powerfully efficient long bow.

One of the interesting stories the museum tells in an exhibit devoted to women in war is of Hannah Snell, who having been deserted by her husband joined the army in 1745 in a vain attempt to find him. She next enlisted with the marines and despite being wounded in the groin during an Indian Campaign still contrived to escape detection. Having finally established her husband's death she turned to a literary and stage career as author of *The Female Soldier*. She later ran a public house in Wapping, appropriately called The Female Warrior. She was duly honoured on her death by being buried at the Royal Hospital Chelsea.

Monmouth grew in importance as it developed under the protection of the Norman castle; it was busy in the iron and timber trade, tanning and in the knitting of Monmouth Caps. The width of Monnow Street, built long before any consideration of the needs of cars was required, demonstrates its centre as a market with the town's manufactured goods exported by river. Daniel Defoe writing in the first quarter of the eighteenth century described the town as "rather decayed" but having a considerable river trade with Bristol.

At the top of Monnow Street is Agincourt Square where a statue of Henry V looks down from the Shire Hall to a statue of another local hero, the Hon. Charles Rolls. The handsome bronze shows Rolls holding a model biplane in his hand. The inscription neatly sums up his many interests "...a tribute of admiration for his great achievements in motoring, ballooning and aviation, he was a pioneer in both scientific and practical motoring, ballooning and aviation and was the first to fly across the channel from England to France and back without landing. He lost his life by the wrecking of his aeroplane at Bournemouth July 12th 1910. His death caused worldwide regret and deep national sorrow". On the plinth three bas-reliefs graphically depict these various activities.

Rolls is further remembered in the museum in nearby Priory Street where photographs show his ascent in 1908 in his balloon "Midget" from the town's gas works. The museum is primarily devoted to a collection of Nelson memorabilia. Nelson, a freeman of the town, visited Monmouth on several occasions and was present at the opening of the Naval Temple on the Kymin. His long naval career is traced in prints, swords, busts, commemorative mugs, some very fine ship models including the Victory and even his alleged glass eye. More grimly there is the log of a ship which Nelson commanded in 1786 which records the punishment by flogging for drunkenness. The dreaded cat o' nine tails lies across the entry.

Lady Hamilton is not forgotten and a pamphlet of the time, price two pence, suggests that the tabloid press is not an invention of our own age. Its rather lengthy title manages to tell the entire story on its cover page thus:

"The astonishing career of a nursery maid, afterwards Lady Hamilton, mistress of Lord Nelson, containing her eventful life from the cradle to the grave giving a full account of her from the period of her first intrigue until the time she became wife of the English ambassador at Naples, the friendly advisor of Lord Nelson, the arbiter of the destinies of Europe and the vicissitudes of her fortune until she died in misery in Bolougne".

The twelfth-century writer, Geoffrey of Monmouth, a native of the county if not the town, and author of *Historia Regum Britanniea*, is said to have been a monk in the Benedictine Priory, now succeeded by St Marys church. Defoe in his brief comments describes the town as Geoffrey's birthplace which had made it famous. Geoffrey was Bishop of St Asaph and later a tutor at Llandaff. His *History of the Kings of Britain* is the base from which the later Arthurian legends grew. The narrative spans the centuries at remarkable length, from 1250BC through the coming of the Romans, Penda's defeat of Oswald and the death of Caedwalla, King of Wessex in AD689.

WYE BRIDGE TO MONNOW BRIDGE

Cross the Wye Bridge and the A40 (subway). Opposite is Monmouth School, founded in 1615 by William Jones, a local man and London haberdasher. The outer wall incorporates the wrought iron gates salvaged from the City of London's Haberdashers Hall, destroyed during an air raid in 1941.

Follow the road as far as the Queens Head (unquestionably the first Elizabeth) where turn left and immediately right to St Marys Street. At the top of the street by the tall spired St Marys church turn left along the stone flagged Church Street to enter Agincourt Square with its old inns, statue of the Hon. Charles Rolls and the Shire Hall where the leaders of the Chartists uprising at Newport were tried.

Follow the broad Monnow Street passing the inn with its stylised sign showing the mounted Henry V in full charge and the Robin Hood said to

A walker passes under the archway on Monmouth's unique bridge
over the River Monnow

be the town's oldest inn. Beyond the cattle market the way slips through the narrow arch of the fortified gatehouse that still defends the Monnow bridge approach to the town. On the western side of the bridge is the church of St Thomas à Becket, an early dedication to the archbishop struck down on the altar steps of his cathedral at Canterbury in 1170.

MONNOW BRIDGE TO LLANTILIO CROSSENNY

From the bridge turn right at the roundabout and follow the B4233 for ¹/₄ mile to turn left on Watery Lane. Keep with the lane for ³/₄ mile. Leave the lane as it bends towards the track to Bailey Pit Farm. Take the path on the right keeping the field boundary (and a stream) to your right. As the boundary curves left cross a stream by a plank bridge and continue with hedge and stream deep below to your right. At the top end of the field turn right dipping through a short patch of woodland to cross a stream by the narrowest of bridges. Beyond the bridge turn sharp left along the field edge to meet and enter Kings Wood, mostly birch, oak and beech. Head steadily west on a clear waymarked path for just over a mile, ignoring all crossing paths and taking care not be be diverted onto the route of a waymarked circular walk. A stone marking the Monmouth parish boundary of 1857 may be noticed en route.

Beyond a gate the ODP follows the inside edge of the wood then continues on a broad track to meet a lane at Lower Hendre. Turn right with the lane and follow it for ¹/₄ mile to join a field path on the left immediately beyond a large modern house. Despite the waymarking there still seems to be some doubt as to the line of the official route and a check on the current signing is recommended. Unless otherwise indicated take a half left course over the field to meet and cross a stile and brook where turn right to follow the hedgerow up a gentle slope. At the next field by a large oak head half left to cross a ditch by a plank bridge. (The River Trothy will be seen in the valley below where the map notes the site of the former Cistercian Priory of Grace Dieu. Some fine long horn cattle may be seen in the fields or a heron rising from the river.) Beyond the bridge maintain your forward direction with a wire fence to your right and clump of hawthorn to your left. Turn right along the fence line to meet a lane near a white house. Turn left with the lane and follow it for 300 yards, crossing the River Trothy by the Abbey Bridge.

Take the path on the right opposite Abbey Cottage heading half right to a stile in a wire fence. Maintain your direction over the field to pass a *barn just to your right. Cross the next field to a stile opposite and beyond a plank bridge turn right to cross a stile into the field that looks down to the Trothy. Bear half left over the field and on reaching the river swing left and on through a gateway. From here follow the bottom of the bank and wood on your left, continuing to pass Sunnybank to your left.*

Just beyond Sunnybank turn left over a stile and turn right on a track which leads to the road opposite St Michaels church at Llanfihangel Ystum Llywern. The church door carries a notice which reads "Offa's Dyke Walkers and others. We would like you to see our church but please respect this House of God and those who worship here. Don't camp, cook meals or leave litter in the church or churchyard, the nearest campsite is Sunnybank Farm." The church was however locked, perhaps they had at last lost patience with those who had made this sad notice necessary.

Take the lane beyond the church passing it on your left to turn immediately left on a path which edges the churchyard, thence over a stile to follow a narrow tread along the side of a stream. Shortly bear right over the stream and up a bank to a stile and over a short field to meet a lane by the former school house. The house has a personalised weather vane showing a teacher reading a book to two children, with a dog paying close attention to the proceedings. All, at the time of writing, live within.

Cross the lane and stile and follow the field boundary to your left. At the top of the field cross a bridge and continue with the boundary to your right until part way up the field a stile takes you into the next field to resume your direction but with the hedge to your left.

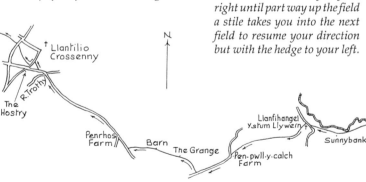

MAP 3/2

As the hedge falls back continue to cross a stile and through a field to meet a lane and turn left passing Pen-pwll-y-calch Farm.

Follow the lane for 600 yards then right on the field path which follows the curving boundary to The Grange. Cross the driveway and over two fields to a stile found to the left of a semi-derelict barn. Thence westwards over a field to cross a stream and onward rising to pass a tree to your right, continuing to return to the lane.

Turn right on the lane, passing Penrhos Farm with its fox topped weather vane and continuing for ³/₄ mile to cross the River Trothy near Llantilio Mill.

A little beyond the bridge turn right through a kissing gate and follow a streamside path, which after crossing the stream, bears left to reach the road via a further kissing gate. Turn left over a bridge following the lane almost to a T-junction (Note the church which is described in the following pages lies to the right of the exit from the fields.)

LLANTILIO CROSSENNY

The village inn, the Hostry, dating from 1459, won the Gwent Pub of the Year award in 1992 and has as its sign an intriguing coat of arms which includes three ladies whose foreheads are bound with writhing snakes. The device will be seen again in the church and connects the village with one of the great characters of history and drama.

The name of the village echoes events of the mid-sixth century when strength of arm and power of prayer combined to defeat an invader. This part of Gwent was ruled over by Iddon whose kingdom was under threat from the Saxons. Iddon sought assistance from Teilo, a saintly man, charasmatic preacher, founder of monasteries, contemporary and travelling companion of St David and later Bishop of Llandaff. A cross was set up, Teilo prayed fervently while Iddon and his men fought mightily and won the

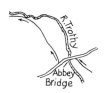

day. In gratitude for the deliverance Iddon gave the church a grant of land where the predecessor of today's church was built.

St Teilo's is a distinguished looking church, remarkably large for the size of the village, and with a fine shingled spire adding 50 feet to the tower. In the church porch there is an exceptionally long parish chest, at least 450 years old with the usual three locks with separate keys held by the incumbent and his wardens.

Within, features of particular interest include the memorial of 1621 set in the chancel floor to a couple and their three children. In the Lady Chapel a carved head on one side of the altar is assumed to be that of Edward II while tucked away on a pillar and easily overlooked is the head of the pagan green man. Near the chapel the coat of arms displayed outside The Hostry is seen again in a window which commemorates Sir David Gam and Sir William Herbert.

Sir David Gam, whose damaged tomb is to be found in Brecon Cathedral, is generally held to be the origin of Shakespeare's Fluellen. His real name was David Llewelyn, but having a pronounced squint was obliged to live with the name that reflected his disability. Although related to Owain Glyndwr he was a loyal supported of Henry IV and received a grant of lands in Wales in acknowledgement of his services in opposing the rebellion.

Gam's support for the crown continued with the accession of Henry V and he took a small band of archers to France in 1415. It was here that he died as he had lived, fighting for the monarch and receiving his knighthood as he lay mortally wounded on the field of victory at Agincourt.

Sir William Herbert, the first Earl of Pembroke, was also a fighting man seeing service in France and knighted by Henry VI. He was a strong supporter of the Yorkist cause during the Wars of the Roses. Edward IV appointed him Privy Councillor and Chief Justice of South Wales in 1461. In 1468 he lay seige to Harlech Castle where Jasper Tudor and the future Henry VII continued to defy Edward's sovereignty. Following the surrender he was created Earl of Pembroke.

In July 1469, William was captured by the Lancastrians at the Battle of Banbury and together with his brother, Sir Richard Herbert, was executed the following day.

LLANTILIO CROSSENNY TO THE WHITE CASTLE

Continuing the ODP from the direction of the church, leave the lane a little short of The Hostry, turning right through a kissing gate to cross two fields

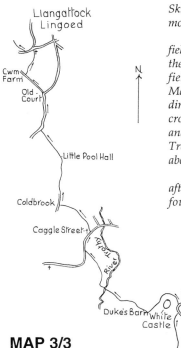

MAP 3/3

with a view to the brown slopes of the Skirrid which will now be in sight for most of the way to Pandy.

Beyond the B4233 head over a field in the direction of the Skirrid and then bear half left through the next field, passing under power lines. Maintain your generally north-west direction over two further fields to cross a stile with trees to your right and continue to the farm lane at Great Treadam. Turn left to meet a lane in about 100 yards.

Bear right on the lane, leaving it after 100 yards to take the wide track found on the right, immediately passing a house and barns to your left. The house has a "hand" as the pointer on its recently installed weather-vane, a left hand as it happens, the builder who drew round his own hand as a model being right-handed.

The lane, generously

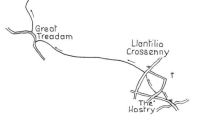

decorated with primroses in early spring, and as it gains height offering some wide views, is followed northwards for ³/₄ mile. At a lane turn left soon passing White Castle Cottage to continue on the "No Through Road" to the White Castle.

THE WHITE CASTLE

The White Castle was one of a trio built by the Normans to secure their hold on this corner of Gwent, the other two being at Grosmont and Skenfrith.

Early in the thirteenth century all three were held by Hubert de Burgh who had been given responsibility for guarding the Marches. By 1205 the castle had fallen into the hands of the notorious William de Braose, but reverted to de Burgh in 1219. De Braose added to a substantial inheritance by conquest from the Welsh but despite King John's rich patronage failed to pay his proper dues to the king and was eventually evicted from his Welsh estates. In 1176 De Braose was responsible for the horrific slaughter of some eighty unsuspecting leaders of the Welsh community. They had been invited to join the marcher lord at Abergavenny castle to celebrate the Christmas season. They were cut down even as they sat at his table in a bloody and cynical abuse of the spirit of peace.

The castle owes its name to the plaster that once covered the walls and which is still partly in evidence today. Considerable improvements were made to the defences in the mid-thirteenth century as the fight for power in Wales continued.

Those who climb the narrow winding stone stairway to the top of the tower can have no doubt of the castle's great strength with its command over a great area of the land. The inner ward, shaped like a Welsh harp was protected by a deep, still water filled moat, drawbridge and portcullis. Military requirements apart the view is superb, particularly to the north with a long prospect to the eastern escarpment of the Black Mountains. Three miles to the west the steep sided 1,594 feet high Skirrid (Ysgyryd Fawr) demands the attention. It is sometimes called The Holy Mountain, a reference to the landslip which is traditionally said to have occurred at the time of the crucifixion. In the south-west lies the Blorenge, just to the south of Abergavenny. The two wireless masts that may be picked out on a clear day are close to the spot where the wonder horse, Foxhunter, owned by Lt.Col.Sir Harry Llewelyn lies buried. This great hearted horse competed at equestrian events throughout the world; among the many prizes he shared with his riders was the Gold Medal at the Helskinki Olympics of 1952.

The deeply moated White Castle Llantilio Crossenny

WHITE CASTLE TO CAGGLE STREET

Leave the tarmac road at the White Castle and take the track which curves round its northern perimeter to meet a stile/gate. Here turn sharp right following the field boundary towards Duke's Barn. Just short of the barn

55

A view to the Black Mountains from the ODP near Pandy

turn right over a stile and follow the field edge for about 80 yards, then left over a stile and sharp right along the hedgeline to a stile at the top of the field.

Descend the field half left (ie. north-west) to a stile, then over a short field to cross the River Trothy. Head to the angle of hedge to follow a boundary on your right to cross a stile at the top of the field. Thence half left over a rising field passing a tree-fringed pond to your left then continuing along the hedge line to meet the road at Caggle Street.

CAGGLE STREET TO LLANGATTOCK LINGOED

Caggle Street is a small ribbon of houses and a chapel, an eastern outlier of the scarcely larger Llanvetherine. Turn right following the lane to just beyond the chapel where turn left over a stile and head half right climbing gently towards trees. At the top of the rise bear slightly diagonally left making for a tree seen on the skyline. Cross the stile to the left of the tree and turn immediately right along the hedge to meet a barn and broad track at Coldbrook. Turn right to follow the hedged lane northwards to a gate then continue through a field to the farm at Little Pool Hall.

Pass the farm to your right to meet a stile and then over rough ground (churned up by cattle) to cross a bridged stream then head up the hillside to meet a lane.

Turn right and follow the lane northwards for 600 yards; violets, wood anemones, dogs mercury, celandine and primrose line the way in spring. As the lane swings to the right, leave it taking the No Through Road, past Old Court and follow this for ¼ mile to Cwm Farm.

Turn right on a broad track crossing a stream. Just beyond the bridge turn left over a streamlet, then bear right to climb the hillside. A stile leads to a narrow path which takes you into the churchyard of St Cadoc at Llangattock Lingoed. (Just short of the gate there is a board advertising accommodation, camping and bunk house at South View.)

The church is a delightfully cool stone building with a barrel vaulted roof and the remains of a fifteenth-century rood screen, intricately carved with interweaving vines. Poppy-head benchends in the chancel and the carved choir stalls carry the date 1634. Extra and less expert embellishments in the shape of the Star of David can probably be attributed to choir boys.

Above the porch a not too easy to read

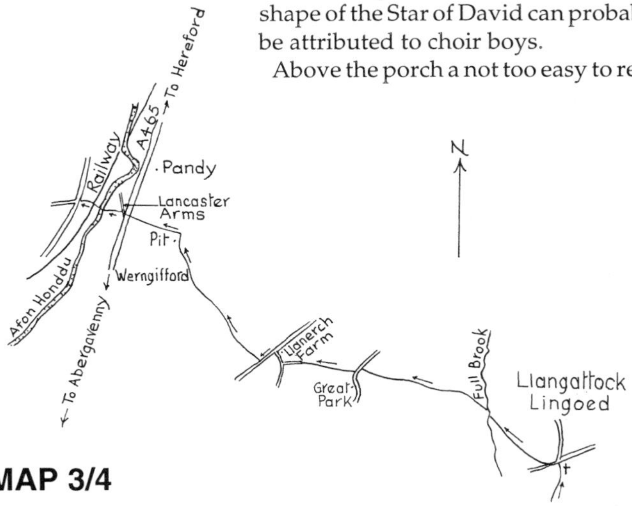

MAP 3/4

tablet records the legacy of Elizabeth Prichard who "...left for the poor of Llangattock 20 shillings to be paid them on St Thomas's Day and charged on a house and a piece of land in this parish with the payment thereof for ever". The excellent church guide details several sons of the parish who made names for themselves in varied careers, including Sir Henry Morgan famed for his buccaneering raids on Spain's West Indian colonies.

LLANGATTOCK LINGOED TO PANDY

Continue through the churchyard to turn left on a metalled lane which soon becomes a rough track with a view to the Skirrid. In 30 yards turn right on a stepped and fenced path to cross a stile and forward over a short field with hedge to your left. Maintain your direction beyond the next stile and in about 200 yards cross a stile and turn right along the hedge for about 70 yards. As the hedge falls back descend diagonally left to pass through a broken hedge and maintain direction to meet and cross the Full Brook.

Beyond the brook head up the steep hillside to cross a stile. Bear slightly left but keeping to the upper part of the hill until you reach a derelict cottage. Here bear diagonally left descending to the stream to cross a stile by a large oak. Continue to the end of the field to reach a lane, where turn left and follow it for 60 yards in the direction of Great Park.

Take the path on the right which climbs close to the field boundary to Llanerch Farm. Pass the farm to your right continuing on a lane to meet the road where bear right. There is a fine view to the Black Mountains with the Sugar Loaf, appearing chad-like, over the hill to your left and the Hatterrall Ridge prominent beyond the valley. On meeting a T-junction in about 100 yards turn left and in a further 100 yards turn right over a stile and head half left over the field to a stile with Pandy seen in the valley below. Maintain your general direction over three further fields, and on entering the next, turn immediately right descending gently along the hedgeline.

At the end of the field cross a stile heading slightly left, to pass a pit, descending to meet and cross a gate. Follow the field edge, to your left, to meet and cross two metal gates in quick succession, thence by a short lane to meet the A465, the Hereford-Abergavenny road.

Cross the road to bear right on a minor lane towards the Lancaster Arms with its promise of refreshments and bed and breakfast.

4: Crossing the Black Mountains
Pandy to Hay-on-Wye

MAPS: 1:25,000 Outdoor Leisure 13 Brecon Beacons National Park Eastern Area (covers to just beyond Hay Bluff)

Pathfinder 1039 (SO 23/33) (small section)

1016 (SO 24/34) (small section but also required for route beyond Hay)

1:50,000 Landranger 161 Abergavenny & Black Mts.

FACILITIES: Shops, refreshments and accommodation at Hay-on-Wye. Camping and accommodation at Pandy, in the Vale of Ewyas on west side of the ridge, near Stanton (off the official route but diversions suggested in text), Llanthony and Capel-y-ffin which also has youth hostel.

PARKING FOR ROUND WALKS: East side of Hatterrall Ridge: Hereford & Worcs CC car park at foot of Black Hill and under Black Darren. In Vale of Ewyas: Queens Head Inn near Stanton has walker's car park, Llanthony, informal off road at Capel-y-ffin, small car park near summit of Gospel Pass and at the stone circle near Hay Bluff.

MILEAGE CHART:

Pandy to Upper Pentwyn		2
Upper Pentwyn to Llanthony/Longtown pass		$2^{3}/4$
(continuation of official route to Loxidge Tump path turn)	(2)	
To Llanthony and return to ridge via Loxidge Tump		3
To Capel-y-ffin turn		$2^{1}/4$
(Descent to Capel-y-ffin (not on official route -	$(1^{1}/2)$	
continuation to youth hostel via Gospel Pass)	(1)	
Capel-y-ffin turn to Hay Bluff		$3^{1}/2$
Hay Bluff to Hay-on-Wye (Oxford Road car park and TIC)		$4^{1}/4$

Total for suggested route $17^{3}/4$

(Official route keeping to the Hatterrall Ridge approx 17 miles)

THE BLACK MOUNTAINS

The Black Mountains fill the eastern bounds of the 519 square miles of the Brecon Beacons National Park. Although not so well known as the very popular central Beacons they have a distinctive character of their own which quickly rewards the walker seeking new territory to explore. The area is thinly populated with its immensely attractive scenery typified by long narrow valleys dotted with isolated farms; steep bracken covered or forested slopes lead on to wild peaty moorland of heather, bilberry and rough grass. A succession of long striding ridges provide superb walking with wide ranging prospects over both England and Wales which may extend for 40 miles or more. Add to this the bonus of some fine skyscapes, good weather and you are set for one of the most enjoyable sections of the Offa's Dyke Path. It is also excellent pony trekking country with several centres along the Vale of Ewyas. Strings of ponies and riders winding their way up the mountain tracks or silhouetted against the light add greatly to the scene and may provide some nicely atmospheric photographs for your souvenir album.

Ravens glide along the scarp edges, an occasional red grouse may be seen skimming low over the heather while buzzards hunt the lower slopes. Hardy Welsh ponies share the grazing with the ubiquitous sheep and may be seen close to the tops in winter when the sheep have moved on to kinder pastures.

The mountains rise to over 2,000 feet, the highest in the range, Waun Fach is 2,660 feet. The ODP crossing of the Hatterrall Ridge, the easternmost of the ridges, touches 2,300 feet. On Hay Bluff, 2,221 feet, you may find that you are sharing your enjoyment with the colourfully equipped aerialists who find the scarp edge an attractive launch point. This fine viewpoint marks the start of a long and rewarding descent to Hay-on-Wye.

In bad weather wayfinding may be difficult for the summit plateaux are often featureless and more distant landmarks disappear as cloud or mist closes in. In these conditions attention to map and compass cannot be neglected nor can reserves of warm clothing, for this open landscape is prey to all the winds that blow, with temperatures sharply lower than in the valleys. In this exposed territory waymarking can be a problem and relics of previous signing which have not stood up to the weather will be noted along

The Black Mountains - a view of the Hatterall Ridge from the hill fort near Pentwyn

the way. Some of the paths are not clearly defined as they leave the ridge but quickly improve to give good descents to Llanthony and Capel-y-ffin on the west and to Longtown and the Olchon Valley on the east. It should be noted that north of the turn to Capel-y-ffin there is no practical way off the ridge on the west until Hay Bluff is reached. Walkers are in any event recommended to keep to the paths indicated on the maps.

Despite these obligatory cautionary words the Hatterall Ridge offers excellent walking whatever the season and perhaps looks its most attractive in the late autumn when the bracken that clothes the hillsides has turned to golden brown. Pick the right day in winter and even this prospect is bettered by a light dusting of snow setting off the still bronzed fern. The heather at this season is dead, not just sleeping but apparently beyond any hope of resurrection but come August it spreads a glorious ecclesiastical carpet of purple over the upper slopes. (Those exploring beyond the ODP might like to note that it is particularly fine around the Bal Mawr ridge to the west of Llanthony.)

There is only one road which goes directly through the Black Mountains, the Gospel Pass. The single track road is a continuation of the minor road that leaves the main Hereford/Abergavenny road at Llanvihangel Crucorney, which after Llanthony and Capel-y-ffin climbs to within 500 feet of the northern scarp between Hay Bluff and Twmpa, otherwise known as Lord Hereford's Knob.

Llanvihangel Crucorney at the southern entrance to the valley can boast the oldest inn in Wales, The Skirrid; it's inn sign depicts the dramatic event when the mountain split in two, traditionally at the time of the crucifixion. The landslip is not unique to the area, the southern end of Hatterrall Hill above Cwmyoy has moved more than once leaving the church standing at a crazy angle and now heavily buttressed to prevent its total collapse.

The full route between Pandy and Hay-on-Wye is described first with the suggested diversion to visit Llanthony Priory following.

PANDY TO HAY-ON-WYE

Once the ridge has been gained the route can quickly be described but the twists and turns of the long steady climb from Pandy to the hill fort which offers some superb views and the equally enjoyable descent from Hay Bluff require rather more detail.

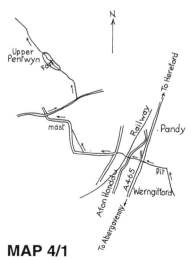

MAP 4/1

Pandy is a small village on the A465. The old market town of Abergavenny, an excellent base for exploring the Black Mountains, is five miles to the south. The cathedral city of Hereford, famous for its early map of the world - the Mappa Mundi - is 18 miles to the north-east, the two connected by rail and bus services. Pandy lies close to the border with England.

The River Monnow whose headwaters are only just in England, forms the boundary for several miles. It surrenders this task in the Olchon Valley to the Hatterall Ridge so that the walker may have one foot in England and the other in Wales. Herefordshire lies to the right throughout, Gwent, which may revert to its pre-1974 name Monmouthshire, gives way to Powys at Capel-y-ffin.

The ODP is joined a few yards short of the Lancaster Arms, turn left over a stile and head directly over a field to cross the Afon Honddu by a narrow bridge. From here there is a long steady climb to the hill fort near Upper Pentwyn which provides a succession of fine views.

Climb the stepped path to meet and cross the railway line and over the opposite bank to follow the field boundary (on your left) to meet a lane. Cross the lane and continue on a narrower rising track which passes Treveddw Farm with its seventeenth-century barn. About 150 yards beyond the farm take the path on the right and head diagonally left over fields in the direction of a wireless mast.

On reaching a lane, turn right to follow it for about 500 yards passing a house and a small pump house with a large cross over the door. The prospect to the left includes the Sugar Loaf seen tipping over the tops of intervening heights.

When a No Through Road is signed ahead, turn right with the lane soon making a sharp descent, with further good views and a visually interesting group of buildings at Brynhonddu.

Five hundred yards from the turning leave the lane to turn left on a good track to reach a gateway. DO NOT GO THROUGH THE GATE *but bear left to follow a narrower hedged path, a hollow way which you may imagine once accommodated the packhorse trains or served as a minor drove from the hills.*

Leave the hollow way by a gate/stile and follow the left-hand field boundary, climbing steeply over the grass and bracken covered hillside which offers a fine view back to the Skirrid.

A clump of Scots pines marks the edge of the hill fort. At a small cairn take the grassy path through the fort area (ie. north-west) leaving the pines to your right. At the far side of the fort the ODP meets a wide track, turn right on this and at the end of the earthworks join the signed and clear grassy way which runs parallel with it.

Before continuing climb the northern ramparts of the fort to its eastern edge. Forward there is fine view of the track running over

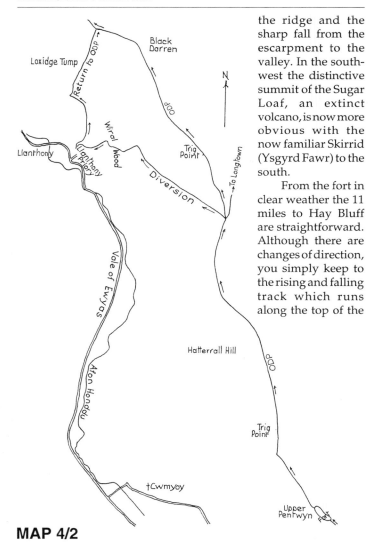

the ridge and the sharp fall from the escarpment to the valley. In the south-west the distinctive summit of the Sugar Loaf, an extinct volcano, is now more obvious with the now familiar Skirrid (Ysgyrd Fawr) to the south.

From the fort in clear weather the 11 miles to Hay Bluff are straightforward. Although there are changes of direction, you simply keep to the rising and falling track which runs along the top of the

MAP 4/2

Offa's Dyke Path looking west - Hergest Ridge
The Whetstone, Hergest Ridge

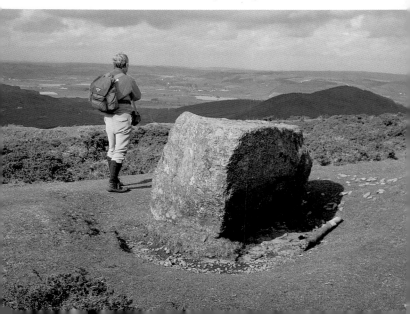

River Wye, Hay-on-Wye

Right:
Herrock Hill,
near Kington

ridge, in places more of a plateau than a ridge. The track is grassy on the lower contours but later deteriorates to black wet peat with perhaps the most squidgy section on the final mile to Hay Bluff. Round walkers should note that some of the paths which leave the crest may be initially indistinct. The featureless nature of the ridge makes the description of reliable landmarks difficult, progress has been measured by signed (hopefully remaining so) paths and triangulation points. With the increasing use of satellite mapping most of the pillars are now redundant and the removal of some is contemplated. Walkers are being encouraged to "adopt a trig point", it is hoped that in upland country such as this, these very useful markers will be allowed to remain.

From the fort the ODP rises steadily passing a large walled enclosure to the left. The first triangulation point, at 1,552 feet, is about ³/₄ mile from the fort. Oldcastle in the eastern valley will be seen far below, identified by the tall Cedar of Lebanon. The Oldcastle path is signed off to the right in just over ¹/₄ mile.

The Llanthony/Longtown crossing is reached in nearly 2 miles - the route is described later. The next triangulation point, 1,811 feet, follows in about ³/₄ mile, from which it is a further mile and a half to the point where the Llanthony diversion rejoins the ODP via Loxidge Tump.

The third triangulation point, 2,001 feet, follows in a mile with views to Herefordshire's Black Hill ridge (2,100 feet at summit) as you advance. A further mile will bring you to the signed Capel-y-ffin (left) - Olchon Valley (right) crossing.

The route continues to the final triangulation point on Hay Bluff, 2,221 feet, reached in 3¹/₂ miles.

It should be noted that about ³/₄ mile short of the Bluff, at Llech y Lladron, the official route veers away taking the bridleway which runs more to the east of the summit, then swings north-west to join the road a little beyond the stone circle.

The more direct track to Hay Bluff is easy to follow, saving the presence of a succession of black peat puddles. About 2³/₄ miles from the Capel-y-ffin turn a short descent is made from higher ground to follow a north-westerly course to Hay Bluff.

Hay Bluff looks out over a wide landscape to the Wye Valley, the Radnor Forest and on a good day the Malvern Hills. *This is the start of a long satisfying but not continuous descent of 4¹/₄ miles ensuring speedy*

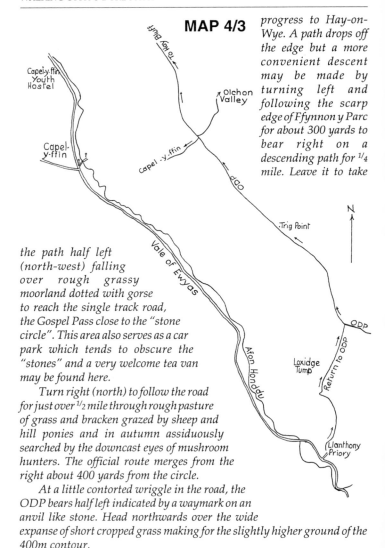

MAP 4/3

To Hay Bluff

Capel-y-ffin Youth Hostel

Olchon Valley

Capel-y-ffin

Capel-y-ffin

ODP

N

Trig Point

Vale of Ewyas

Afon Honddu

ODP

Return to ODP

Loxidge Tump

Llanthony Priory

progress to Hay-on-Wye. A path drops off the edge but a more convenient descent may be made by turning left and following the scarp edge of Ffynnon y Parc for about 300 yards to bear right on a descending path for 1/4 mile. Leave it to take

the path half left (north-west) falling over rough grassy moorland dotted with gorse to reach the single track road, the Gospel Pass close to the "stone circle". This area also serves as a car park which tends to obscure the "stones" and a very welcome tea van may be found here.

Turn right (north) to follow the road for just over 1/2 mile through rough pasture of grass and bracken grazed by sheep and hill ponies and in autumn assiduously searched by the downcast eyes of mushroom hunters. The official route merges from the right about 400 yards from the circle.

At a little contorted wriggle in the road, the ODP bears half left indicated by a waymark on an anvil like stone. Head northwards over the wide expanse of short cropped grass making for the slightly higher ground of the 400m contour.

MAP 4/4

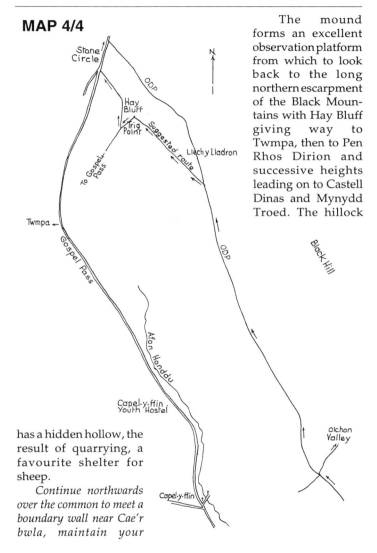

The mound forms an excellent observation platform from which to look back to the long northern escarpment of the Black Mountains with Hay Bluff giving way to Twmpa, then to Pen Rhos Dirion and successive heights leading on to Castell Dinas and Mynydd Troed. The hillock has a hidden hollow, the result of quarrying, a favourite shelter for sheep.

Continue northwards over the common to meet a boundary wall near Cae'r bwla, maintain your direction with the wall to your left as Tack Wood closes in from the right. The path is funnelled into a V angle to meet and pass through a gate after splashing through a trickle of spring water.

Beyond the gate bear right up a bank and through a broken wall to continue with a fence to your right and the stream on your left. In a short distance the rocky bed of the stream is crossed to meet a broadening track passing Cadwgan Farm on your left. Continue with the track now deep between bank and hedges.

About ¼ mile from the farm leave the lane as it bends to the left, taking the path on the right, descending steeply to woodland. As the line of trees is met turn right on a clear path and in 50 yards sharp left down the hillside to meet a lane.

There is yet another fine vista over the wide landscape of this delightful border country, with an improved but ribbon like view of Hay ahead with perhaps a glimpse of the Wye in the valley before the hills beyond claim the attention. Nearer at hand buzzards quarter the falling ground and the staccato drilling of woodpeckers mingles with the bleat of sheep.

Turn left along the lane and in a few yards turn right over a stone stile to descend two fields and part way along the boundary of a third to cross the deep cleft of a stream.

Here turn left descending by the tree fringed stream which provides a sheltered haven heavily populated with blue and coal tits, to meet a lane and turn left. In just over 300 yards, take a stile on right, bearing diagonally left toward a clump of trees. From the trees bear left along boundary to a stile, descending to cross a plank bridge with the Dulas Brook tumbling over waterfalls to your right.

The brook which forms the boundary between Wales and England is the subject of an old legend which recalls a bloody battle with the Normans on the hills above Hay in 1093. It was claimed that the slaughter was so great that the little stream ran red with blood for three days. A story that may have been inspired by the reddish soil through which the tributary which has just been crossed runs and in time of spate will add its colour to the water.

Beyond the bridge continue forward. From here the way to Hay is clear with an easy crossing of several fields via kissing gates, some of which are a mite small for a walker with a rucksack never mind a fully laden back packer.

MAP 4/5

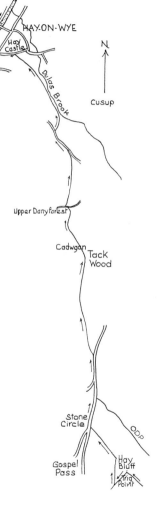

The field paths bring you to a lane which in turn leads to the main road, where turn left to the main car park, information centre and toilets.

DIVERSION TO LLANTHONY PRIORY

The Llanthony/Longtown crossing path is found nearly 3 miles north of the Pentwyn hillfort. For Llanthony turn left and take the good track which descends north-west for ³/₄ mile, then levelling out as it swings more to the north following boundary to your left for about ¹/₄ mile. Here turn left over a waymarked stile descending along the field edge to enter Wiral Wood.

Bear half right on a good falling track through the wood to enter a field by stile. There is a superb view of the valley from this spot, Llanthony Priory lies below with the hills rising sharply on both sides of the narrow road. Gerald of Wales described the valley as three bowshots wide. Beyond the Priory the deep cleft of Cwm Bwchel splits the hills with the top of Bal Mawr seen beyond. Southward the grim cliffs of Darren are in sombre contrast with the woodland and pasture they overlook.

Turn right to follow two sides of the field to meet and cross the stile in the far corner. Follow a dry stone wall curving left round the enclosed area and through gates to reach the Priory and the little church of St David.

LLANTHONY PRIORY

A small community is gathered here in the narrow valley walled in by the hills clustered around the fine but roofless Priory at Llanthony or to use its full Welsh name, Llanddewi Nant Hodni. Herein lies the clue to its history for the reference is to the church of David by the river. David, patron saint of Wales, died in AD601. He gained a reputation as a teacher, traveller, founder of monasteries, and, as some were ready to suggest, as a miracle worker. He is said to have travelled to Jerusalem with St Teilo where they were both appointed bishops.

Traditionally it is believed that David visited this remote valley and established a small chapel or hermitage which indirectly led to the founding of the Augustinian monastery early in the twelfth century. William de Lacy a member of an influential family happened upon the now ruined chapel and retired here to live the life of a hermit. William was shortly joined by the Queen's chaplain, Ernisus, and others who together built the first church. From this grew the Priory whose great arched windows still frame a view to the hills.

Archbishop Baldwin visited the Priory in 1188 in the course of his six week journey through Wales seeking recruits for the third crusade to Jerusalem. He was accompanied by Giraldius, Archdeacon of Brecon, usually referred to as Gerald of Wales, who kept a careful diary of their travels. Little seems to have escaped Gerald's sharp eye and busy pen. He was clearly impressed with Llanthony, although not with all who lived there for he writes of the steady theft of the community's property by successive priors. He devotes several pages in his *Journey through Wales* to the founding of the Priory and to a description of the countryside. He particularly commends it for the healthy climate and the suitability for the practice of religion.

With the dissolution of the monasteries the building inevitably fell into decay. In AD1809 the estate was acquired by the writer Walter Savage Landor, author of *Imaginary Conversations,* with the intention of pursuing the life of a gentleman farmer. An insight into his character is indicated by his expulsion from Rugby School and the enforced curtailment of his studies at Oxford. His time in Llanthony was all too short for the proper development of his agricultural ambitions. Lacking sufficient capital and beset by debt he was obliged to leave the valley to live abroad.

Close to the Priory is the parish church. A simple stone building, furnished with the smallest of towers to house its single bell and within a recently installed stained glass window depicting St David. Here he is seen bearded and bright eyed with the dove of peace upon his shoulder. On his right is the little church which bears his name and to the left the greater building of the Priory, with the hills beyond.

Three miles upstream just before the narrow road starts its long climb through the hills lies Capel-y-ffin - "the chapel on the boundary". Here is another, even smaller community, Chapel Farm and a barn by the roadside with a scatter of houses and farms on the hillsides.

An old stone wall and yew trees surround the church of St Mary's. The white walled, stone tiled church is topped by a tiny turret set at an angle that surely defeats the builder's intentions. Inside a small gallery looks down to the wooden pulpit from which sermons have been preached for over 200 years. Within and without all is simple but quietly impressive.

Along the lane is the Baptist chapel, not usually open, with a plaque that records how William and David Prosser "brought the ministry of the gospel to their house in the year 1737".

On the western slopes of the valley, near the pony trekking centre at The Grange, is the monastery, Llanthony Abbey, founded in 1860 by the Reverend Joseph Lyne, who adopted the name Father Ignatious. This man, a powerful preacher by all accounts, was ordained into the Church of England but his teachings were in conflict with established practice of the day. The construction of a chapel was begun; incomplete it remains as a memorial to its founder who is buried beneath its roofless walls.

In the 1920s the monastery buildings were acquired by Eric Gill, the artist, typographer, sculptor and carver who established a small community of artists here. Gill will be remembered for his widely used typeface, Gill Sans-serif. His sculptures include the Stations of

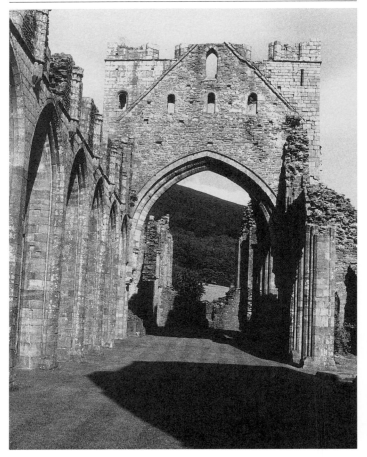

Llanthony Priory, Vale of Ewyas

the Cross to be seen in the nave of Westminster Cathedral and the figure of Ariel on the BBC building in Portland Place. There is a small chapel in an upper room above the former monastery that is normally open to visitors with a portrait of Eric Gill near the top of the stairs.

RETURN TO THE ODP VIA LOXIDGE TUMP

From the Priory take the field paths northwards (initially waymarked out of the valley as far as the wicket gate below an old quarry) passing to the east of Loxidge Wood, then by a twisting path which climbs above the quarry, thence north-eastwards on an increasingly indistinct path to rejoin the ODP on the 600-metre contour.

DESCENT TO CAPEL-Y-FFIN

The Olchon Valley/Capel-y-ffin paths are signed 2 miles north of the Loxidge Tump path. For Capel-y-ffin turn left to meet a boundary stone with the improving path falling south-westerly with good views down the valley. The route has been waymarked to Capel-y-ffin from the stile found in the fence line roughly above the Vision Farm. A descent is made via woodland, thence by a lane, field paths and a further track to meet the road just beyond St Marys church at the foot of the Gospel Pass. A further mile of road walking is required to reach the youth hostel.

With the long period of sometimes intensive, not to say fervent, religious activity in the area speculation on the events which lead to the naming of this road through the mountains can explore many avenues. An old legend claims that St Peter and St Paul came this way after the crucifixion. Add to this St Davids fifth-century chapel, Llanthony Priory, the churches, chapels and monastery at Capel-y-ffin, the perambulations of Archbishop Baldwin and there is more than adequate reason for the name whatever the true origin may be.

5: In the steps of the Drovers
Hay-on-Wye to Kington

MAPS: 1:25,000 Pathfinder   1016 (SO 24/34) 993 (SO 25/35)
         1:50,000 Landranger   148 Presteigne & Hay-on-Wye

FACILITIES: Shops, refreshments and accommodation at Hay-on-Wye
    and Kington. Post office/shop, accommodation and camping Gladestry.
    Some other possibilities en route.

PARKING FOR ROUND WALKS: Oxford Road car park, Hay-on-Wye.
    Kington Town Centre or informal at top of Ridgebourne Lane, Kington
    for Hergest Ridge etc.

MILEAGE CHART:
Hay-on-Wye to Newchurch   6½
Gladestry   3½
Kington   4¼

Total   14¼

This section follows the official route throughout.

After leaving Hay there is a pleasant section of level walking
alongside the Wye and through farmland before the ODP takes to
the hills again with a long steady climb that begins from the A438
near Bronydd. A crossing of the eastern edge of the Little Mountain,
Disgwylfa Hill and the Hergest Ridge all offer fine views. There is
excellent walking throughout, good underfoot and a great feeling of
airy freedom from the grassy moorlands. Although a rising and
falling route, peaking at 1,400 feet the gradients are not demanding
and this section might comfortably be completed within the day.
Refreshment, apart from a single water tap, is unlikely to be found
before the inn at Gladestry.

The attention of those planning their own round walks is drawn
to the permutations available on the Hergest Ridge at the Kington

end. Walkers based at Hay might like to consider walking out to Gladestry and taking a taxi back - this will have to be summoned from Hay and some preliminary arrangements are advised.

HAY-ON-WYE

At Hay-on-Wye we exchange one diarist for another. Although they lived some seven centuries apart they seem to have much in common; both were clerics, both had an eye for the countryside and recorded what they saw. The first we have already met, Gerald of Wales, Archdeacon of Brecon and clearly an early travel writer. The second, the Reverend Francis Kilvert, was for much of his ministry a curate and although he was appointed to his own parish his death from peritonitis at a relatively early age leaves open the question of how far his career in the church might have advanced.

He knew this border country well, serving as curate in nearby Clyro, then as vicar of St Harmons to the north of Rhayader. He was vicar at Bredwardine, a Wyeside parish a few miles downstream from Hay from 1877 until his death in 1879.

The literary baton had already been handed over before we reach Hay, for Kilvert was a great walker and in his diary we read of his walking over the hills to Capel-y-ffin and his first meeting with Father Ignatius. He clearly made a great impression on Kilvert who confided a detailed description of the monk to his diary, with references to his saintly face and earnest expressive eyes.

Kilvert was a regular visitor to Hay and his diaries are peppered with references to the town, of fairs, market days and social visits to the castle. The reader threading his way through Kilvert's daily writings gradually pieces together a picture of life in this border town when the railway had arrived but agriculture and social practices were not so very different from those of preceding centuries.

Hay's history is a long one but the visitor is more likely to be concerned with its present than its past. This old market town now offers something very different from the livestock that was driven here along the dusty roads or the cheese, butter and eggs sold by the farmers' wives at the Butter Market. Hay has become, quite extraordinarily, the centre of a large second-hand book trade with over twenty-five or so specialist and antiquarian book and print sellers.

Book browsers beneath the walls of Hay Castle

Not that you need to be any sort of specialist to enjoy the book-shelves of Hay. You may browse away quite happily on a rich and varied diet that ranges through every aspect of fiction, science, art, history, military matters or whatever, at prices that are as wide ranging as the subjects themselves. Many of the shops are open seven days a week, and exterior shelves with adjacent honesty boxes provide a twenty-four hour service.

Much of the trade is centred in the little tangle of streets and alleys that lie around the castle, not its first castle but its second. Built around AD1200, in a single night if local folklore is to be relied upon, it and the town were soon suffering all the distress and indignities of the border area. King John attacked the castle in 1216 during the Barons War following his wilful neglect of the terms of the Magna Carta agreed at Runnymede the previous year. Llywelyn ap Iorweth the Prince of Gwynedd and Lord of Snowdonia, otherwise known as Llywelyn the Great, left the castle a smoking ruin in 1231 as part of his campaign, first against John, and then Henry III to maintain his independent rule.

Henry had the castle rebuilt in 1233 and the security improved by the construction of the town walls a few years later. It was not a peaceful century. Henry III and his son Prince Edward were, like his father John, in trouble with the Barons who were still trying to limit the sovereign's powers. Prince Edward stormed the castle in 1264, the year that Simon de Montford took Henry prisoner at the Battle of Lewes. De Montford, effectively the power behind the throne, inflicted great damage on Hay Castle in 1265, as he campaigned to subdue opposition from across the Welsh border. Prince Edward escaped from imprisonment at Hereford and joined forces with Llywelyn ap Gruffydd. After much manoeuvring along the border, Edward defeated de Montford and his supporters at the Battle of Evesham. De Montford died on the field of battle, peace followed and in 1267 Llywelyn was formally accepted by Henry III as Prince of Wales by the Treaty of Montgomery.

Hay was plundered early in the fifteenth century during Owain Glyndwr's campaign against the English Marcher Lords with the castle in ruins long before it could be pressed into service during the Civil War of the 1640s. It might have totally decayed had not the gatehouse become a private residence.

The town would have developed around its first castle of which only a green mound, to be seen near the parish church, remains. Within the church there is a curious and much worn effigy, possibly of a monk, but said to be that of Maud Walbee, otherwise Maud de

St Valerie, wife of William de Braose II. She it was, "they say", who laboured so mightily to build the castle in the course of a single day.

The temptation to linger amongst the bookshelves of Hay and to make a leisurely bookish perambulation before setting off on the day's walk is obvious and not one that I would wish to discourage. For those who have already made a literary circuit or two and now require a quick getaway the following route is suggested.

HAY TO THE WYE BRIDGE

From the Oxford Road car park turn left passing the Craft Centre to turn right into Castle Street. Here the old fire station carries a plaque commemorating Richard Booth's first bookshop, the start of the now famous second-hand trade in the town. Take the left turn, Beaumont Road, B4350, passing the Clock Tower, obligatory it seems for Welsh towns. Thence next left

MAP 5/1

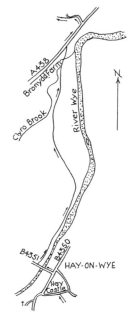

signed Clyro 1 mile passing The Three Tuns, one of the town's oldest inns, which still retains its mounting block to assist the arrival and more probably the departure of its horse borne patrons.

The Wye here is wide and often shallow, a delightful sparkling river tumbling over a rocky bed. As you cross the bridge you may pass other walkers coming into Hay as they complete the first 36 miles of the Wye Valley Walk from Rhayader. Hay is also the starting point for the 100 mile, three day raft race to Chepstow.

At the far side of the bridge turn right to follow the river downstream for just over ½ mile on a clear path through trees. To your left on the hillside near Boatside Farm the map indicates a Roman fort but nothing of this can be seen from the ODP.

The path descends to a clearer view of the river where a stile is crossed to continue through a field with the path running near the Wye. At the end of the field, cross a stile and head slightly left edging away from the river. From the next stile bear left along the hedgeline to meet a gateway beyond which turn immediately right on a broad track between hedges, with the white houses of Bronydd seen clustered on the hillside above the main road.

Just before a further metal gate is reached turn right over a stile and then left to cross a field with the hedgeline a little to your left. Currently blue marker circles have been installed by the landowners to supplement the ODP signing.

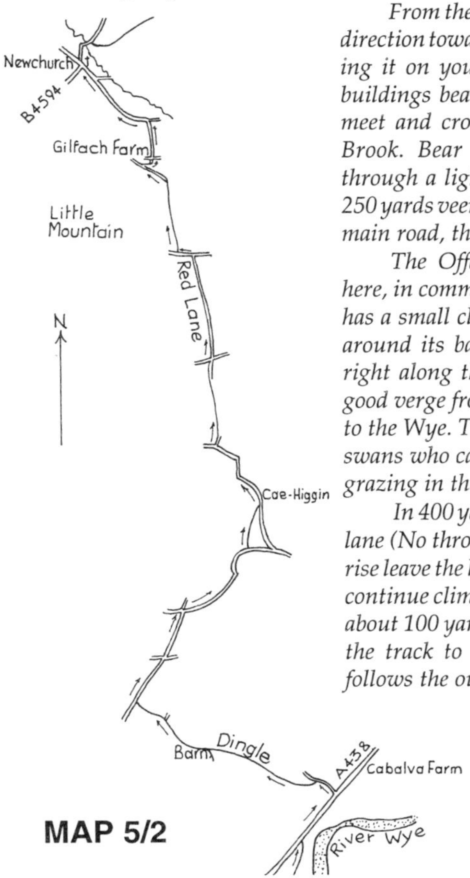

From the next stile maintain your direction towards Bronydd Farm, passing it on your left. Beyond the farm buildings bear half left over a field to meet and cross a stream - the Clyro Brook. Bear right from the stream through a lightly wooded area and in 250 yards veer left up a bank to meet the main road, the A438.

The Offa's Dyke Path signpost here, in common with other road signs has a small clump of daffodils planted around its base - a nice touch. Turn right along the busy road but with a good verge from which there are views to the Wye. This is a favourite spot for swans who can be seen on the river or grazing in the fields.

In 400 yards turn left on a narrow lane (No through road). At the top of a rise leave the lane by a stile on the left to continue climbing on a rutted track. In about 100 yards bear half right leaving the track to take a clear path which follows the outside edge of the wooded Bettws Dingle with the Cabalfa Brook hidden in the deep ravine to your right.

The remains of the farm buildings of Cwm-

MAP 5/2

bwllfa are seen on the hillside to your left and later the large stone New Barn. In a while the path descends through the plantation to cross the stream. Continue through the woodland on a steepening path with the bedrock occasionally underfoot. (Note the left and right turns should be ignored.)

As you reach the top of the rise bear left, up a bank and sharp left on the path which terraces the hillside high above the stream. (Note again the path to the right to Upper Bettws should be disregarded.)

Emerge from the darkness of the woodland to climb a stepped path to meet a lane about 400 yards north-east of Tump Farm. (A sign on the path currently advertises camping at the farm.)

Turn right with the lane. A fair amount of height has been gained, we are now on the 850 feet contour, with wide views over an open landscape to the distant foothills of the Black Mountains. In ½ mile at a road junction turn right, signed Rhydspence 1½ miles and keep with it for nearly ½ mile.

As the road curves to the right by a house, turn left over a stile and go forward over a rising field. From the next stile bear half right, passing an ancient oak and making for the stile by the cream painted farm house. There is an improved retrospective view to the misty bastions of the Black Mountains.

Turn left along the lane, passing the entrance to Pentwyn House. In 300 yards, as the lane bends to the left by the bungalow at Cwm-yr-eithin, turn right initially on a narrow path hemmed in by gorse and bracken to meet a gate. Beyond the gate the path broadens to a wide green lane, a characteristic drove way.

Later as we cross Disgwylfa Hill and the Hergest Ridge the droves follow high open country but here, for at least some period, the cattle and sheep were contained by the hedgerow. The drovers trekked out of Wales for centuries, quite how long does not seem to have been fully defined. Some writers mention the early fourteenth century, others indicate a time span from the eleventh to the coming of the railways, a full 700 years. And what a journey it was, crossing the hills, fording the rivers, later dodging the tollgates where they could, heading for Shrewsbury, Birmingham, Hereford and London. At a rate of 10 or 12 miles a day it was a long and tiring journey for the drovers and their charges. Time had to be allowed for wayside grazing and good overnight accommodation found for the beasts which both fed and contained them. No good pushing the

Sheep from the drove road near Newchurch

herds and flocks too hard to speed up the journey, the loss of quality in tired underfed animals would quickly be reflected in the price. A poor sale reported to the farmers on the return would soon put an end to the drover's career. Indeed some of the drovers would have invested their own money in the flock and would be doubly anxious to secure the best possible price. Kilvert's village of Clyro was one of the places where drove roads converged after the crossing of the Wye. Upstream important crossings of the river were made at Rhayader, Newbridge where the ford used since Roman times can still be seen, Erwood where the toll house remains by the modern bridge and at Builth Wells.

On the hillside to your right the map indicates Pen-twyn Settlement in the gothic lettering the Ordnance Survey reserves for ancient monuments.

The green lane climbs steadily to fine views over the high rolling pasture, then dips to meet a metalled road beyond a gate. Cross the road to continue on the initially metalled lane and maintain your direction on Red Lane for nearly 1/2 mile, for a while following the boundary between Herefordshire on your right and Powys. At the top of the lane, bear half left and in a short distance turn right along the fence line heading north.

The ODP is now crossing the eastern flanks of the Little Mountain - summit 1,167 feet. The track that has just been left continues towards another enclosure although it is not clear from here what its purpose might have been (quite likely a collecting point for livestock).

Kilvert writes of walking over the Little Mountain and in one

Descending towards Newchurch

entry noted the activities of the lapwings. On another occasion in a nice turn of phrase which I leave readers to discover for themselves, he revels in the glowing glory of the gorse. Later he complains of the cutting down of some birch trees, intolerantly and uncharacteristically laying the blame with an unnamed baptist. He was on his way to Newchurch where he seems to have been a frequent visitor and on another of his treks over the hill he extols the magnificent view. We too enjoy the scene of a rolling countryside, here reminiscent of the South Downs.

Keep with the fence line on your right, as the ODP heads northwards. Beyond a gateway, continue along the boundary on springy turf, over a further stile to make a steady descent still along the fence line. Newchurch is seen below and to your left the 1,400 feet high Newchurch Hill.

The track curves down the hillside towards the farm at Gilfach-yr-heol, once farmed by a former rector of the parish and his family. Near the bottom of the hill and just short of the farm, fishook right and in 30 yards turn left on a hedged lane. Pass through a metal gateway on to the lane and continue your descent to meet the road where bear left to Newchurch.

Goats graze in the churchyard at Newchurch

NEWCHURCH

This is a tiny village on the infant River Arrow, very much a farming settlement with a few houses and stone barns and proud of its award for the best kept village in the Radnor District, 1989. Great

House is passed to your right as you come to St Mary's church with goats tethered to the tombstones and engaged in keeping the churchyard grass under control. Once the churchyard boasted an 1100-year old yew but it fell in January 1990. Nothing of any great moment could possibly happen here you might think. The passage of the drovers coming over the hills from Painscastle as they headed for Kington might have caused a temporary stir on their way through the village. Perhaps they paused for refreshment at the village inn or made an overnight stay bringing news of the outside world.

One traveller who was long remembered was Charles II, who could hardly be missed since he came this way at the head of an army. He paused at the farm at Blaencerde on the hill above the village and, seeking refreshment, was provided with a jug of milk. The story and the jug from which a king drank were handed down and 200 years on reached the ears of Kilvert who duly recorded the incident.

Within the church is a memorial to the Reverend David Vaughan, for 17 years curate and 33 years rector. It was he that farmed at Gilfach-yr-heol and Kilvert delights in telling that arriving unannounced he found the rector's attractive daughters sharing in the somewhat gruesome work in hand - castrating the young lambs.

NEWCHURCH TO GLADESTRY

At the small crossroads beyond the church turn right, signed Kington, shortly passing the old Sunday School of 1848. Just before the quarry from which most of the village was built, take the path on the right. To your left is a private residence, once The Oak Inn, and to your right the blacksmith's forge closed during the 1940s; more recently the village lost its post office.

Beyond the house go ahead on a rising path to meet a metal gateway. Beyond, the ODP climbs north-eastwards over the open country of Disgwylfa Hill, clothed in grass, bracken and gorse. As the fence to your right falls back maintain your direction to the first summit (1,187 feet), with the occasional concrete post marking the way. Continue over the crest of the hill, dipping down to a crossing path and a small pool before climbing again on a clear grassy track between bracken and over the next "summit" (1,256 feet). There are fine airy views here and birds picking ticks or wool from the sheep's backs.

Towards the bottom of the slope turn sharp left on the wide track which leads to a gate and continues to pass Hill Farm. Here a tap set in the wall offers refreshment and an encouraging verse for Offa's Dyke Path walkers.

Keep with the farm lane to a road junction and turn right passing Grove Farm. In 200 yards take the path on the left following a wire fence over a short field to meet a stile. Cross the next field, slightly right, following marker posts to a stile thence continuing northwards along the field boundary (on your left) to meet a road opposite the entrance of Freshfields. (Note this appears on some maps as Stonehouse Barn and a change from the original line of the ODP has been made to take the route a little away from the house.)

Turn right and in 40 yards turn left on a fenced track. As Freshfields is approached bear right up the hillside following the fence line to the top of the field. Turn left over a stile and follow the field boundary (to your right). Turn right through a small enclosure to join a lane with the Hergest Ridge seen ahead. Keep with the descending track and part way down the hill as it levels out turn sharp right by a large tree, then almost immediately left descending over grass with a disused quarry to your left and stream to your right.

In 200 yards turn right crossing the stream to a stile. Bear left over the stile to meet the road by a barn and turn left to reach Gladestry in ½ mile.

GLADESTRY

Gladestry is another village lying beneath the hills with the

MAP 5/3

steep slopes of Yewtree Bank glowering down upon it. Just a little larger than Newchurch and still managing to retain its own school and village inn.

The church of St Mary boasts a flying dragon on its weather vane and within a small parish chest dated 1692. There is a memorial to Captain Basil Bickerton Evans which records distinguished service during World War I; He was decorated for his work with the British Military Mission in the Balkans, by the King of Greece. The village forge is now an antique shop.

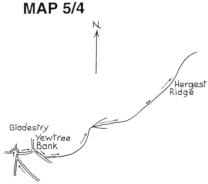

MAP 5/4

GLADESTRY TO KINGTON

On meeting the junction at Gladestry turn right following the road to cross a small river, passing Court House of 1689, the Zion Chapel of 1842 and the Royal Oak. Beyond a second stream turn right signed Huntington 1½ miles and follow the road for 200 yards then bear left on the gated "No Through Road".

The lane climbs steadily with the sharp slopes of Yew Tree Bank to your left. Beyond "The Camp" the metalled lane gives way to a good stony track leading to the open hillside. The way over the Hergest Ridge is variously indicated with stout signposts, concrete fence posts and low plinths.

Shortly after passing the first of the waymark posts three tracks are encountered, take the middle one, a fine grassy way which climbs through bracken.

As height is gained there is a view to the Black Mountains and the full run of the Hatterrall Ridge; more distantly to the Brecon Beacons identified by the great scoop of Arthur's Chair between Pen-y-Fan and Corn Du. Even Worcestershire's Malvern Hills can be seen on a good day. To the north-west are the heights of the Radnor Forest with Black Mixen, 2,132 feet, marked by the tall wireless mast. It is not the peak of the range, this honour falls to a

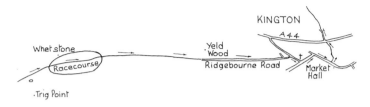

slightly higher plateau, 2,165 feet, more to the west above Great Rhos.

There are two ponds, like the dew ponds of Sussex, on the ridge, the first is passed on the 400-metre contour. The ODP does not go directly over the, 1,397 feet summit but curves gently to pass it on its northern side. The wooded Hanter Hill, with extensive quarrying beyond, is seen to your left and the second pond is reached on the plateau below the summit.

From this point it is about 300 yards to the ellipse of the racecourse, a splendid place for a gallop. The ODP cuts through the centre of the course but you can briefly follow its northern track to the Whet Stone. This squarish block of rock is supposed to have served as a "trading post" during the plagues of the fourteenth century. Here farmers left wheat for collection by the quarantined townsfolk. An awkward and unusual location, for transactions of this nature were more frequently conducted by a stream bordering the afflicted town or village. Rather more common is the legend attached to the stone that at dawn it leaves the hill to drink from a stream.

The ODP is easily regained by a narrow tread through the heather with the stout post that marks the way clearly visible. A new marker has now appeared, the imaginative planting of a small group of monkey puzzle trees that will soon be visible to travellers from afar.

Continuing over the ridge, descend through the loop of the racecourse with Bradnor Hill coming into view and the rooftops of Kington gradually revealed. Beyond Bradnor Hill the shapely Titterstone Clee Hill curves northwards towards Brown Clee Hill, the highest point in Shropshire.

The directly eastward descent leads to a gateway by Yeld Wood and on to Ridgebourne Road which is now followed for ³/₄ mile. On reaching the road turn right and bear left at a junction, passing the church, to follow Church Road descending to the centre of the ancient market town of Kington.

6: Back to the Dyke
Kington to Knighton

MAPS: 1:25,000 Pathfinder   993 (SO 25/35)
          971 (SO 26/36)   950 (SO 27/37)
          1:50,000 Landranger   148 Presteigne & Hay-on-Wye

FACILITIES: Shops, refreshments and accommodation at Kington and
    Knighton on route and at Presteigne off route.

PARKING FOR ROUND WALKS: Formal car parking in Kington town
    centre and at Temeside picnic site, Knighton. Some off road parking
    possible at spots along route.

MILEAGE CHART:

Kington town centre to Burfa Bank	4¾
Burfa Bank to Dolley Green	4
(Note nearest spots to Presteigne are from point where ODP crosses minor road near Evenjobb or at next road near Castlering - 3 miles)	
Dolley Green to Knighton	5¼
Total	14

This section follows the official route throughout.

In this section of the walk the ODP rejoins the dyke which hasn't
been seen by the traveller since leaving it in Highbury Wood near
Redbrook some 55 miles back. The dyke's course in the intervening
miles has been somewhat fragmented with sections appearing near
English Bicknor in the Wye Valley and the possibility that Hereford's
Row Ditch may have formed part of Offa's work. Beyond Hereford
a section ran from the loop of the Wye into Garnons Wood. Other
stretches have been identified on the ground in the Lyonshall area
well to the east of Kington with the ODP making a junction with the
dyke on Russock Hill two miles north of the town. The dyke
continues over the 1,228-foot summit of Herrock Hill, with the ODP
forsaking it to make a descent along its eastern flank. From thereon
the ODP is on or near the dyke most of the way to Knighton. At some

points it is no more than a shallow bank, at others impressive despite the relentless passage of a dozen centuries with the height from bottom of ditch to dyke top ten feet or more.

The labour and planning required to construct the earthwork demanded a substantial commitment of which the biggest cost would have been the man hours - whether payment was made to willing workers or the enforced labour of local "recruits" who might have felt happier tilling their fields or tending their flocks. I asked a civil engineer how much the construction might have cost in today's money. Without a seconds hesitation he replied, "Tell me the total cubic feet of earth to be moved and I'll give you an estimate". Given the varied nature of the terrain and the considerable difference in the height of the bank I decided not to pursue the calculations any further.

The way between Kington and Knighton continues across the grain of the land, dipping and rising to provide a succession of often wide ranging views. The finest of these, given the right lighting conditions, is the superb prospect to the west of the wild hills of the Radnor Forest.

KINGTON

Kington is an old market town in the north-western tip of Herefordshire with ODP travellers crossing the boundary into England about $^1/_4$ mile beyond the first pool on the Hergest Ridge. A mildly interesting situation since it is clear from the line of the dyke to the north and east of Kington that this put the site of the town beyond Offa's Mercian kingdom, while Presteigne, which is only just in today's Wales, lies some 3 miles to the east of the dyke.

Hergest, a mile to the south west of Kington was the home of the Vaughans, a well known Welsh family. Thomas Vaughan held various appointments at the hands of Lancastrian Henry VI and in 1460 was charged with the responsibility of seizing for the king some of the border estates of the Duke of York and the Earl of Warwick. Later he gave his allegiance to the Yorkist cause, a change of horses for which he was to pay with his death at the Battle of Banbury in 1469. His descendants continued to live at Hergest and gave great encouragement to the Welsh poets and writers of the day. It was here that the Red Book of Hergest, a collection of Welsh

Kington parish church

folk stories and mythology was discovered and translated by Lady Guest as *The Mabinogion* in the 1840s. A work counted all the more worthy for she was not Welsh by birth and only studied the language after her marriage to Sir Josiah Guest, the Merthyr Tydfil ironmaster.

On a hill overlooking the town and almost aloof from its parish is the church of St Mary the Virgin, a distinctive building with a large, almost detached tower, topped by a tall shingled spire. The white alabaster tomb of Thomas Vaughan and his wife Ellen can be seen in a side chapel. The folklore of the area ascribes some strange, not to say horrific, stories to Thomas, "Black Vaughan" as he became known. Vaughan was said to have been a man of such wickedness that death's long sleep did not calm his spirit so that he returned in various manifestations to the annoyance and downright fear of the local population. It seems that every misfortune of life came to be attributed to the ghost of Vaughan, if a waggon overturned on the way to market, then sure enough it was his doing. If a horse, irritated by a persistent fly, reared up in anger it was Vaughan's evil work. The stories multiplied all too easily and there were tales of the devil's footprints appearing in the fields, his sulphurous tread burning the grass so that it never grew again. When he assumed the form of a black bull and entered the sacred precincts of the church it was judged time to exorcise his evil restless spirit. It was, we are asked to believe, no easy job requiring the combined forces of twelve priests each armed with the traditional accompaniments of the service of exorcism, bell book and candle. After a mighty struggle they contrived to confine Vaughan in a snuff box which was thrown into a pond there to lie, so they say, for 1,000 years.

Close to the church is the Grammar School, founded in 1625 by Lady Hawkins, second wife of the famous Elizabethan buccaneer Sir John Hawkins. His adventurous, but by no means entirely virtuous, career included slave trading, the plundering of Portuguese ships, command of a ship during the battle with the Spanish Armada and later Treasurer of the Navy.

The architect employed to design the school was John Abel, a specialist in timber framed buildings, although this was not one of them. He was a man of considerable talents and during the siege of Hereford by the Parliamentarian forces during the Civil War invented a machine to mill corn. His resourcefulness impressed Charles I who appointed him the King's Carpenter. Abel died in his nineties and is buried in the churchyard at Sarnesfield where the epitaph he wrote for himself can still be seen on his table top tomb.

Kington continues its long history as a market town with sales of sheep and cattle, a reminder that Herefordshire sheep were particularly well regarded. Reference to the "Leominster Ore" has been made earlier, an expression which may have its origins in the mid fifteenth century. It was claimed that the finest wool came from Leominster, a parliamentary document of 1454 referred to its value as £13 per sack, wool from the Shropshire march came next at about £8; from the remainder of Herefordshire a sack commanded a price of £5.6.8 (£5.33 in today's money) with Sussex wool said to be worth only £2.10s. (£2.50).

Brecon born, Sarah Siddons (1755-1831), the theatrical darling of her day, launched her career in Kington as a member of a touring company managed by her father Roger Kemble. Her later Shakespearean roles on the London stage included Portia in *The Merchant of Venice* and Lady Macbeth.

Kington today still reflects its past with a number of old inns dating back to the coaching age. The town was on the mid-Wales Worcester to Aberystwyth route via Rhayader and part of a network of stage coach routes which connected the principal towns. The advent of the railway put an end to what many today regard as a romantic era, but coach travel was long, hard, difficult and uncomfortable, fraught with many hazards not the least the often poor state of the roads and the danger of being robbed along the way. The growth of the turnpike, now so often recognised by the toll houses along their course, shortened journey times and in turn encouraged an increase in travel. In some ways a forerunner of the motorway age, but first came the tramway.

The tramway, ancestor of the railway, was a single line commercial route designed to improve the transport of heavy goods, notably coal from the mines of South Wales, which was transferred into horse drawn waggons from the barges of the Monmouthshire and Brecon Canal. The initial line, from Brecon to Hay, was working by 1816 and four years later it had been extended via Eardisley and Lyonshall to Kington and the quarries three miles to the north-west of the town.

Kington earned its daily bread not only from the passing trade but from rural industries. From the sheep to the west it developed the manufacture of cloth while the richer cattle country of Herefordshire provided the hides for tanning and gloving. The

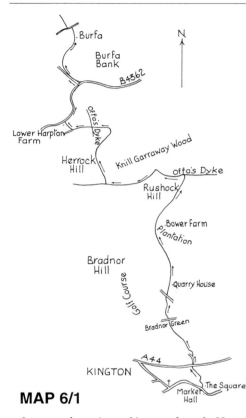

MAP 6/1

Back Brook, crossed on our way, out of the town, fed the mill race to power a local foundry near today's roundabout on the A44.

Leaflets from the Information Centre in Mill Street and the excellent church guide provide more detail of Kington's past but it seems there is still one mystery waiting to be solved - which king was it that gave the town its name?

LEAVING TOWN - KINGTON TO THE A44 FROM THE MARKET HALL VIA THE CHURCH

If the parish church of St Mary the Virgin has not already been visited, head up Church Street - the route of your inward journey from the Hergest Ridge. On leaving the church retrace your steps a short distance to take the public footpath on the left which descends steadily to meet and cross the Back Brook by the A44.

VIA THE SQUARE

From the market hall head up Church Street passing the Castle Inn and turning right into The Square. Bear left and beyond Walnut Gardens, take the descending road which soon passes the National School of 1836. Continue over the junction to the No Through Road known as Crooked

93

Well. A strange name apparently derived from an old superstition that a bent pin thrown into the well as payment would ensure a cure for diseases of the eye.

The road dips to meet a row of white painted cottages alongside the Back Brook beyond which a bridge and the busy A44 is crossed.

KINGTON A44 TO REJOIN THE DYKE ON RUSHOCK

Cross the A44 to the signed path opposite, passing Engine Cottage to your left. Take the rising narrow lane and just short of a five barred gate turn sharp right through a spiked gate crossing a garden-like field in front of the Rhue Ville farmhouse. This serves as a nursery for young lambs who in spring graze amongst the daffodils - a pretty picture combining the two elements of the season.

Make for the wooden gate to pass the house to your left and continue on a wide hedged track. At the end of the lane a kissing gate leads to a crossing of a field with retrospective views to Kington which improve as further height is gained. Beyond a further kissing gate follow the hedged path which leads to Bradnor Green and its scatter of enviously located cottages.

Some 340 acres of common land on Bradnor Hill (summit 1,283 feet) is owned by the National Trust and accommodates a golf course, said to be the highest in Europe: a course in which the wind must on many occasions play a significant factor in the final totting up of the score card. Lofty courses are not unusual in this western part of England, Cleeve Hill near Gloucester is well over the 1,000-foot mark and there is a challenging course above Shropshire's Carding Mill Valley which must run Bradnor Hill's record pretty close with one corner at around 1,230 feet.

Cross a track and go forward to pass a white house with tall trees in its garden to your right and over a further track with the club house seen away to your right. Maintain your direction to meet a notice which warns walkers to watch out for golfers using the fairway. Go directly ahead to cross this danger zone. At the top of the rise cross a metalled lane and continue beyond a cattle grid on the lane which leads to Quarry House.

Leave the metalled track in about 80 yards, turning left along the fence line and soon curving half right to the top of the field by a long strip of woodland. Beyond the stile continue with the woodland to your right, passing a sheep fold.

As the trees peter out bear half left to a stile seen ahead, level walking here with a view to the flat topped Rushock Hill. Beyond the stile, head slightly left over the field to a further stile with the farm buildings of The Bower seen beyond the fir plantations to the north. Cross a further stile and continue with the path rounding the outside of the western end of the plantation to a further stile.

From here make for the diagonally opposite corner of the field (ie. north-west) to meet a metal gateway and stile. Now head directly up the hillside to meet the fence line and continue with this on your right. At the top of the field cross a stile set in a wire fence and as the fence on your right falls back, continue over Rushock Hill to meet Offa's Dyke and turn left with it.

RUSHOCK HILL TO BURFA BANK

The dyke, with some pronounced changes of direction, is now followed for nearly ¾ mile with views opening out to the hills in the west and Bradnor Hill to the south. Whilst only of modest height it is clear enough on the ground and would have left the people of the day in no doubt that it was the boundary set by Offa to his kingdom.

A wide track is joined as Herrock Hill becomes more prominent. Beyond a stile and gate leave the track to follow the dyke for about 100 yards, then turn sharp right leaving the dyke as it continues along the southern side of Herrock Hill. There are a number of paths in the Herrock Hill area but the ODP is well waymarked as it heads northwards with the woodland away to your right. In about 100 yards bear half left on a grassy descending track which follows the very steep eastern flanks of Herrock Hill.

The view to the west is now blocked by the great bulk of Herrock Hill but to your right there is a fine prospect up the valley of the Hindwell Brook. The wooded Wapley Hill, about 4 miles to the east is the site of a hill fort and is yet another of the suggested locations for Caractacas's last stand against the Roman legions.

The path falls to join a track coming in from the right, maintain your northward direction on the now fenced and hedged track which passes the buildings noted on the map as Herrock Cottage. The track curves westwards passing Croft Plantation on your right with its fine stand of tall sturdy oaks which give way to conifers as a gateway is reached.

It is at this point that Offa's Dyke may be noted as it descends Herrock

Hill and continues through the plantation to cross the valley bottom.

Remain with the track to pass a cream painted house to your left. In about 150 yards cross a stile on your right and bear left to follow two sides of a large field, passing the buildings of Lower Harpton Farm to your left and on to meet the road.

Turn right, crossing into Powys once more, and follow the road for about 600 yards. Shortly after crossing Ditchyeld Bridge turn left on a minor road as you reach the Forestry Commission's Burfa Bank plantations.

BURFA BANK TO THE EVENJOBB ROAD

Shortly join the forest road found on your right and as it curves to the right in about 100 yards, leave it to go forward on a narrower track on the inside of the wood with open country to your left.

This area has long been occupied by man, on the forested hilltop, and out of sight is a large elongated hill fort. Further to the west near Hindwell Farm the map shows the square outline of a Roman Fort, close by at Womaston there is a motte and bailey of the Norman age. Indeed wherever the eye makes a casual exploration of the map there are references to standing stones, tumuli, mottes, pond bays, four stones, all in that special Gothic script with which the cartographers pay respect to the relics of past ages.

The track widens as it passes Burfa House which has a plaque that records a date from the fourteenth-century. Beyond a second house the track reaches a metalled lane; turn left with this and in about 50 yards turn right over a stile. Climb the short bank and bear immediately left along the top of the dyke.

The dyke is now followed north-westerly for nearly ³/₄ mile, swopping from one side of the fence line to the other as indicated by the waymarked stiles, with a gentle almost unnoticed gain in height.

The road is reached to the right of the plantation on Evenjobb Hill. The village lies nearly ¹/₂ mile to the west.

Presteigne, just inside the Welsh border, can be reached by road, 3 miles to the east, with shops refreshment and accommodation. The next two road crossings also provide connections to the town. Presteigne, now part of the much larger county of Powys, was once the county town of Radnorshire and reputed to have been the smallest assize town on either side of the border. The town is said to have a somewhat uncertain connection with John Bradshaw, the

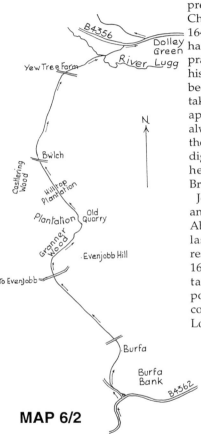

MAP 6/2

president of the court that tried Charles I in Westminster Hall in 1649. Bradshaw could hardly have been called the leading practitioner of jurisprudence of his day and it must only have been the reluctance of others to take on the task that led to his appointment. The King, who always rejected the validity of the court, behaved with great dignity despite the aggressive, hectoring behaviour of Bradshaw.

John Bradshaw died in 1659, and was buried in Westminster Abbey, but it was not to be his last resting place. With the restoration of the monarchy in 1660 his body was exhumed to take part in a bizarre posthumous punishment. His coffin, together with those of the Lord Protector, Oliver Cromwell, and Henry Ireton, were hanged at Tyburn and their bodies burned: an act of barbaric symbolism impossible to justify today whatever their crimes may have been.

EVENJOBB TO BWLCH

At the road turn left for a few paces and then take the path on the right into Granner Wood. Go ahead for a few yards then sharp right climbing a wooden ladder to the path above. Here turn left on a narrow but clear rising and occasionally stepped path to meet a forest road. Cross the road and continue, north-easterly, still gaining height and with a steep fall to your left.

Leave the wood by a stile and go ahead on a grassy terraced path which soon climbs a bank to meet a track. Turn left, passing a quarry on your right and just beyond, by a corrugated iron barn, turn sharp right up the steep hillside to the stile seen ahead. From here head north-west with a wire fence and hedge to your right, the dyke is present but not impressive. The way climbs gently to continue through Hilltop Plantation with the dyke gaining a little height.

On leaving the wood continue with the now falling dyke, passing the farm at Pen Offa well to your left (a fallen notice bears the legend "Camping Pen Offa"). A hillfort (1,075 feet) crowns Castlering Wood to your left as you continue along the dyke to meet the road at Bwlch (another chance to head eastwards to Presteigne if required).

BWLCH TO DOLLEY GREEN

Cross the road to continue with the dyke, initially to your left, heading a little east of north, rising steadily before descending to meet the next road in ¾ mile.

There are some fine views along the valley of a shapely landscape with here and there a crown of trees topping the hills. To the west a view to the Radnor Forest sometimes afforded an air of dignified mystery as the clouds sweep low over the tops. Forward beyond the valley of the Lugg, Furrow Hill draws the eye to the next climb. The dyke grows in stature with the height from ditch bottom to bank top as much as 15 feet in places.

The stile which leads to the road is invisible until the last moment and is found at the end of the dyke.

Presteigne can be reached by following the road eastwards for just over 2 miles or from the next crossing at Dolley Green.

Cross the road to the gate and stile opposite and bear right to follow the field edge with a stream to your right. The ODP has now left the line of the dyke which has suddenly vanished from view although traces can be seen on the map and its course is rejoined on Furrow Hill. At the end of the field cross a stile and continue to reach the River Lugg. Bear right with the river heading downstream along a sometimes muddy track to reach and cross an iron and concrete bridge.

The Lugg has its source 10 miles to the north-west high on Pool

A view to the hills of the Radnor Forest from Furrow Hill

Hill, and continues via Presteigne and Leominster to join the Wye at Mordiford a few miles south of Hereford.

Continue beyond the bridge with a hedge to your right to join a rutted track which meets the road (B4356) shortly after passing through a gateway.

The small village of Whitton lies along the road to the left. Nearby, Pilleth carries the memory of a battle of 600 years ago. Crossed swords mark the spot on the map between the River Lugg and the rising ground just to the south of the modern road. The principal players on this bloody stage were Sir Edmund Mortimer, a member of an influential family; Owain Glyndwr engaged in a growing campaign against the Marcher Lords; Henry IV; Henry Percy, Earl of Northumberland, and Richard II, already dead but whose fate was still something of a mystery.

Edmund was the youngest son of the 3rd Earl of March, who had served as Marshall of England for 8 years and ambassador to France. A strange circumstance surrounded his birth at Ludlow in November 1376 for it was whispered that on that day the Earl's horses had been inexplicably discovered in their stables knee deep in blood. This was taken as a portent of a future disaster but it is not clear whether this omen was recognised only in hindsight and thus became a self fulfilling prophecy.

The future Henry IV, Bolingbroke, had been banished from England in 1398 as a result of his opposition to Richard II. He returned in July of the following year intent on overthrowing the king and seizing the throne, Edmund; perhaps with an eye to the main chance, indicated his loyalty. Richard who had been absent in Ireland returned to face surrender, confinement in the Tower of London, abdication and within a few months, death in Pontefract Castle either murdered or from self inflicted starvation. His fate does not seem to have been generally known and there was some lingering hope that perhaps he was still alive.

In June 1402 Glyndwr launched a determined attack on the Radnorshire area, establishing a base near Pilleth. With the Mortimer estates under threat, Edmund collected together a sizeable army of Herefordshire men and his tenants - Welsh of course. It seems that advancing towards Pilleth, he chose to ignore conventional military wisdom by making an attack on Glyndwr who was already in possession of the high ground. Gross ignorance, reckless abandon or something more sinister? Whatever the reason the English inevitably suffered many casualties; estimates vary between 200 and 1,000. Some of the Welsh tenants, pressed men no doubt, took off and others more sympathetic to their fellow countryman turned their bows on Edmund's men.

Edmund was taken prisoner but treated by Glyndwr rather more as a guest than a prisoner. Attempts by the Percy family to secure his release on payment of a ransom, as was the custom of the day, did not go well and Henry IV, fed on the suspicion that there might be more in the matter than met the eye ordered an end to the negotiations and underlined the point by seizing Mortimer's treasures.

Mortimer duly converted to Glyndwr's cause and sealed his new allegiance by marriage to his daughter Catherine. He publicly announced his intent to assist in the restoration of Richard and failing that to attempt to place his (Mortimer's) nephew, the young Earl of March on the throne.

The Percys who had supported Henry also changed their allegiance and in 1403 were allying themselves with the Welsh under Glyndwr. The inevitable clash of arms took place just outside Shrewsbury. It seemed at one time that the King's forces might be defeated. Certainly casualties were heavy on both sides, but the death of Henry Percy, "Hotspur", proved to be a decisive moment in the battle and Henry's throne was secure for the moment. The outcome might well have been different had Glyndwr been able to join forces with Hotspur but they were heavily committed in west Wales. Hotspur's death had been forecast years earlier when a soothsayer had predicted that he would die in Berwick and he not unnaturally assumed it to be the northern border town. He had however slept the night before the battle at a small village not far from Shrewsbury. Incredibly his sword was left behind, as he led his army towards the battlefield he discovered not only its loss but that the village he had just left was called Berwick.

And what of Edmund Mortimer? In 1409 he and his wife shared with Glyndwr the deprivations of the long seige of Harlech Castle. Edmund died like so many of the garrison of starvation, Glyndwr somehow contrived to escape.

DOLLEY GREEN TO B4357 JUNCTION

Turn right along the road to Dolley Green, a pretty name which surely can't be real, conjuring up pictures of a rosy cheeked country girl or a fairy tale location: a tiny place with a scatter of houses and a little church.

Just before the sign which announces the village take the hedged track on the left which climbs steadily. In ½ mile the hedges fall back and a gate leads onto the open hill. Remain with the clear track as it curves up the hillside with the fence line to your right. At the top of the field cross a stile by a gateway and continue with the track in the direction of (but not into) Gilfach Wood with improving views of the Lugg valley and the little village of Whitton to the west and the hills beyond.

As the wood is neared bear right with the track to meet a stile and metal gate. Remain with the track with the wood well to your left. At the next gate as the track begins to fade away into the grassland of Furrow Hill bear diagonally left to meet the fence line and continue northwards with it crossing further stiles and rejoining the dyke.

The south-western view to the wild heights of the Radnor Forest

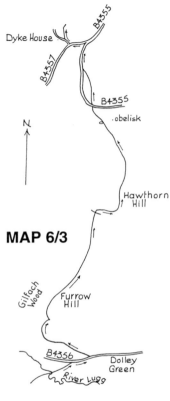

MAP 6/3

is superb. Despite the reference to forest it is only partly wooded and provides some good walking with a succession of hills over 2,000 feet.

The ODP continues northwards with the fence switched to the right beyond a stile. Just after passing a ramshackle barn with its loose corrugated iron sheeting flapping in noisy protest in response to every breeze that blows, a change of direction is signed. Turn right over a stile, heading east along the fence line, soon dipping through a soggy patch.

In 300 yards turn left over a stile and resume your northward progress, with the fence to your left, and a little to the west of the summit of Hawthorn Hill (1,335 feet). At the top of the field cross a stile and go ahead with the fence line to your right.

Continue with the boundary, and the dyke, to your right, for ½ mile. As a plantation is reached turn right over a stile and resume your direction with a wire fence on your left and the plantation on your right.

Cross a stile into an open field and go forward with fence and another plantation to your left.

On a small rise forward right, off the route, is a polished stone obelisk, a laudatory pencil pointed to the sky. The inscription reads: "This public monument was erected by subscription to perpetuate the memory of Sir Richard Green Price, 1st baronet, born 1803 died 1887, for services to the county of Radnor which will long outlive his name. Through his untiring energy the railway to Knighton and Llandrindod was constructed as well as to Presteigne and Radnor...".

MAP 6/4

The lower part of the tribute is now difficult to read.

As the plantation falls back cross the stile on your left and bear half right passing a gorse fringed pool, then over a driveway to join a path at the fence line where turn right soon to meet the road (B4355). Cross to a stile and maintain your direction with the boundary to your left and Scots pines along the dyke, to rejoin the B4355 in a little over ¼ mile. Turn right with the road and in 400 yards left at the junction with the B4357 (note Knighton is signed right 2 miles). In 200 yards leave the B4357, turning right on a minor road.

B4357 TO KNIGHTON TOWN CENTRE

The ODP continues northwards to Knighton keeping to the edge of a succession of fields, boundaries swopping from left to right and back to left as progress is made and with some good sections of the dyke.

Follow the minor road for about 40 yards then turn right over a stile and immediately left along the field edge. After crossing short fields the dyke is rejoined and followed to your right over fields. A steady rise brings you to trees at the top of a field, turn right over a stile and immediately left to continue with the dyke and fence line to your left.

The wooded hills beyond Knighton come into view and a brief stretch of level walking provides an eastward view to Titterstone Clee and Brown Clee Hills. The ODP continues with Great Frydd Wood to your left and the greens of the golf course to your right.

A steepening descent leads into the woodland; in about 60 yards turn left over a stile bearing half right. In 30 yards the path divides; take the left path which falls to meet and cross a tarmac path beyond the wood. Go forward on a narrow fenced path with a view over Knighton, St Edwards church on a hillock and the modern red brick houses in strong contrast with the white painted stone cottages of earlier centuries.

A stile is crossed where bear right behind houses and in a few yards left into Frydd Terrace and shortly right on the main road and almost immediately left to descend to the car park. Pass through the car park and under an archway into the town centre. Turn left up Broad Street to the clock tower thence up West Street to the former school which now houses the youth hostel and the headquarters of the Offa's Dyke Association.

7: Teme to Clun
Knighton to Newcastle

MAPS: 1:25,000 Pathfinder   950 (SO 27/37)

                                  930 (SO 28/38)

         1:50,000 Landranger   137 Ludlow & Wenlock Edge

FACILITIES: Shops, refreshments and accommodation at Knighton and
    Newcastle and off-route at Clun.

PARKING FOR ROUND WALKS: Knighton and informal off road at some
    junctions with path.

MILEAGE CHART:

Knighton to Selley Hall	3¼
Selley Hall to Lower Spoad	4
(Note Clun is 3 miles to the east via B4368)	
Lower Spoad to Bryndrinog	½
Diversion to Newcastle	½

Total   8¼

This section follows the official route except for the optional diversion to
Newcastle for refreshment or accommodation.

The crossing of the hills from Knighton to the Clun valley provides
some of the best sections of Offa's Dyke. As it follows the western
side of Llanfair Hill the dyke reaches its highest elevation about
1,411 feet if the triangulation point a little to the south is taken as a
measure. The earthwork which disappeared on the descent to
Knighton is briefly re-discovered in the park behind the Heritage
Centre. After the steep climb to Panpunton Hill the dyke is followed
or is in sight for virtually the whole of this section with some fine
views both of the Teme and Clun valleys as well as to more distant
and perhaps less easily identifiable points.

The suggested itinerary is on the short side for a full day's

The Teme valley from the ODP

walking but is included to provide some flexibility. The next town of any size close to the route is Montgomery, over 18 miles distant, so that those travelling to join the route at Knighton will probably appreciate a half day's walk. Those who have journeyed from Chepstow will already have covered some 80 miles and may be glad of a shorter day. YHA members booked in at the Clun hostel have to allow for a diversion off the route of 3 miles. For a few miles beyond Newcastle accommodation possibilities close to the ODP are not easily found.

KNIGHTON

Knighton, in the valley of the Teme, lies beneath the steep slopes of Kinsley Wood and is only just in Wales. Its name in Welsh is Trefyclawdd - The Town on the Dyke - so it is appropriate that the headquarters of the Offa's Dyke Association are located here,

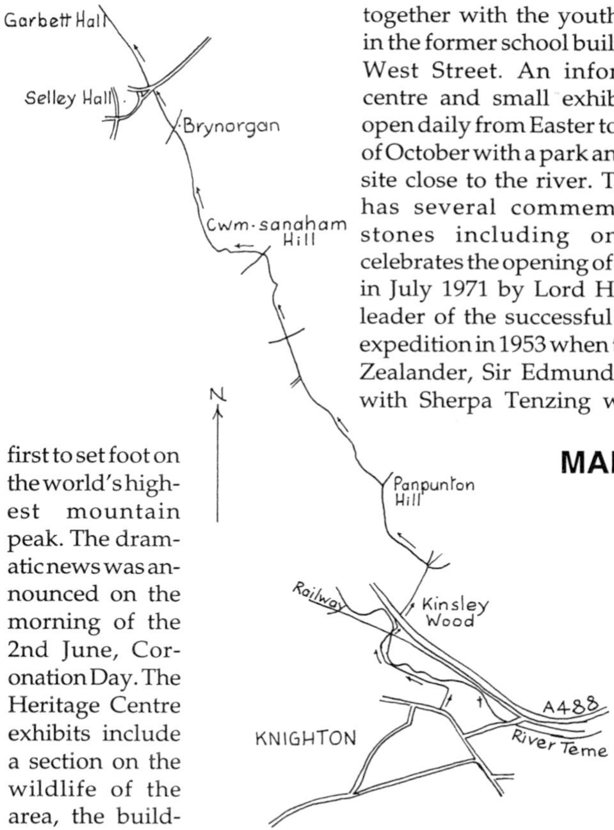

Garbett Hall

Selley Hall

Brynorgan

Cwm-sanaham Hill

N

Panpunton Hill

MAP 7/1

Railway

Kinsley Wood

A488

River Teme

KNIGHTON

together with the youth hostel, in the former school buildings in West Street. An information centre and small exhibition is open daily from Easter to the end of October with a park and picnic site close to the river. The park has several commemorative stones including one that celebrates the opening of the path in July 1971 by Lord Hunt, the leader of the successful Everest expedition in 1953 when the New Zealander, Sir Edmund Hillary with Sherpa Tenzing were the first to set foot on the world's highest mountain peak. The dramatic news was announced on the morning of the 2nd June, Coronation Day. The Heritage Centre exhibits include a section on the wildlife of the area, the building of the dyke and a rather splendid silver foil portrait of Offa created by the pupils of Osbaston School in Monmouth.

Another long distance walk starts from Knighton, Glyndwr's Way. The 120 mile route lies entirely in Powys and crosses the county westwards via Abbeycwmhir and Llanidloes to Machynlleth, where Glyndwr as Prince of Wales held a parliament in 1404. The Way then makes an easterly curve to Welshpool to link with the Offa's Dyke Path and thus provides a full circuit back to Knighton.

To return to the ODP. There are no great stories from history to recount save for the building of the dyke and that has already been dealt with, no churches along the way with interesting memorials, no spicy tales that I have been able to discover with which to regale readers. Just the fine border landscape, with sheep on the hills, buzzards soaring high in the skies above and the dyke rolling determinedly northwards as it has done these last 1,200 years. Step out and enjoy.

KNIGHTON TO SELLEY HALL

From the Clock Tower go forward on West Street and on the assumption that the Heritage Centre has already been visited, turn right down Crabtree Lane. At the foot of the lane turn left through the car park and picnic site and follow the path upstream, before long leaving Wales to enter Shropshire. The path follows the River Teme for just over ¹/₄ mile before crossing it by a footbridge and then over the railway track. Continue to a stile and in 50 yards bear right to a further stile to meet and cross a lane to a metal gateway.

From here the ODP climbs steeply on a wide track with the northern boundary of Kinsley Wood a little to your right. At the top of the slope turn sharp left, north-westerly, soon passing a fir plantation to your right.

There is a fine view up the valley where the Teme takes a meandering course with the railway making a beeline for Knucklas to head westwards as it seeks a way through and indeed under the hills.

Beyond the plantation the path narrows with the fence line kept to your right and stiles to be crossed at intervals. When a broad crossing track is met turn right and then immediately left to continue with the dyke. At yet another plantation a stile transfers the path to the western side of the fence line.

The path follows the outside of the woodland and dips to cross a bridleway before winding up the hillside to the triangulation point on Cwm-sanaham Hill.

From the trig point cross a stile to continue with the dyke. As the fence falls back the path swings half right and downhill to a stile. Beyond the stile a narrow path falls steeply, marked by posts, and with a good view ahead to the dyke seen running up the far hillside towards Llanfair Hill.

The path falls to pass the white painted house, Brynorgan, and continues to meet a lane near Selley Hall.

ODP from above Brynorgan with the dyke climbing ahead to Llanfair Hill

SELLEY HALL TO LLANFAIR HILL

A stile leads to a short steep climb, with the dyke to your right, to a clump of larch trees. Go forward on the dyke soon losing height and after crossing a broad track go ahead to a plank bridge built by the Royal Engineers, then on to another bridge and stile to meet the road by Garbett Hall.

Cross the road and through a gateway to bear right past farm buildings. From here on the way is clear as you take a broad rising track which runs close to the dyke lined with larch trees and dotted with clumps of gorse. The dyke steadily improves as do the views. After levelling out for a while the ODP crosses a track soon to follow the dyke to the summit triangulation point just off the bank at 1,410 feet and reached in just over a mile from Garbett Hall.

Continue with the dyke for about ¼ mile until a fence bars your way and a conservation notice directs you to leave the dyke and join the track on the left which has been running parallel with the dyke for some while.

LLANFAIR HILL TO SPOAD HILL

The farm track is followed northwards for well over ½ mile with the dyke rolled out like a great green hose over the hillside, seen perhaps as the Welshmen of 1,200 years ago might have viewed it from their side of the border.

The wide track is also the route of another trail - waymarked with discs of a bridle route - the Jack Mytton Way. There are fine views to west and east with a brief glimpse of the Long Mynd, Wenlock Edge and Titterstone Clee Hill to the right and the Welsh hills beyond the Teme valley.

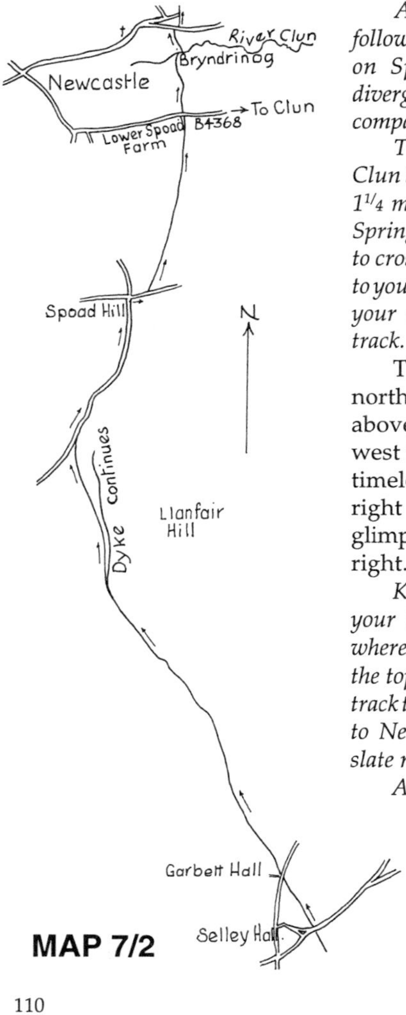

MAP 7/2

At the minor road turn right and follow this for ³/₄ mile to the crossroads on Spoad Hill, with the initially diverging dyke returning to keep closer company with the road.

Turn right at the crossroads signed Clun 3³/₄ miles to the right (Newcastle 1¹/₄ miles ahead). In 200 yards, at Spring Hill Farm, turn left over a stile to cross a short field with a plantation to your left to a further stile to continue your northward descent on a broad track.

There are superb views, northwards as the dyke rises again above the Clun Valley and north-west to Newcastle set beneath the timeless hills. As the bank to your right falls back there is a further glimpse to the Long Mynd, forward right.

Keep the fence line and dyke to your left to the bottom of the field where cross a stile and go ahead along the top of the dyke now with the farm track to your left and with a closer view to Newcastle with its white walled, slate roofed houses.

As you near Lower Spoad Farm, cross a stile by a large oak and bear half left for a few paces then turn right on the track which leads through the farmyard to meet the road, the B4368.

Newcastle and the Clun Valley from Spoad Hill

CLUN

Clun, with youth hostel, accommodation, shops and refreshments, lies 3 miles to the east. It is an attractive village with an ancient five-arched bridge over the river and an even older but now ruined castle. The stumpy remains of this once important border castle stand on a high mound overlooking the village. Built in the years following the Norman Conquest the castle and the village below suffered the inevitable slings and arrows of the outrageous fortunes of the border territory: double trouble since it came under attack by the Welsh and by King John during the Barons War.

St Georges church, a mainly Victorian restoration but with some Norman work is seen across the valley on a site that once accommodated a Bronze Age settlement and pre-Conquest churches.

Sir Walter Scott visited the border country in the 1820s and it is believed that the castle may have been the inspiration for the Garde Doloureuse in *The Betrothed* published in 1825. Along with three other villages, Clunton, Clunbury, and Clungunford, Clun is described as one of the quietest places under the sun in A.E.Housman's *A Shropshire Lad*, not far wrong, but there is another candidate for this honour which will be discovered as the Offa's Dyke Path moves on.

THE WALK CONTINUED

Those not heading for Clun should turn left at the lane and in a few paces right over a stile. The farm seems to have been built directly over the dyke which puts in a further brief appearance before vanishing as the floor of the valley is crossed.

Descend with broken fence line to your right to meet a gateway and stile and follow the field boundary, on your left, as it curves to meet and follow the River Clun. The river is crossed by the very fine half timbered house at Bryndrinog.

Bear left beyond the bridge and then right to pass a barn. Immediately beyond the farmyard turn sharp left up the hillside to join the dyke soon to reach the road to the east of Newcastle.

Newcastle, yet another small village, is set in the valley of the Clun, with post office, shop, refreshments, inn and accommodation.

Fine timber framed house at Bryndrinog by the River Clun

8: Crossing the Oldest Road
Newcastle to Montgomery

MAPS: 1:25,000 Pathfinder   930 (SO 28/38)
                                    909 (SO 29/39)
         1:50,000 Landranger   137 Ludlow & Wenlock Edge

FACILITIES: Shops, refreshments and accommodation at Newcastle and
    Montgomery (diversion from the official route). Bed and Breakfast on or
    near route, also at Clun 3 miles off route and Church Stoke 1½ miles
    off route.

PARKING FOR ROUND WALKS: Official car park/picnic site on edge of
    Montgomery. Some verge side parking may be possible near Newcastle,
    Churchtown and the Kerry Ridgeway but most of the lanes are very
    narrow.

MILEAGE CHART:

Newcastle to rejoin ODP	½
(From Clun 3 miles)	
Newcastle to Churchtown	3¼
Churchtown to Kerry Ridgeway	1¾
(Bishops Castle to the east via road 4½ miles)	
Kerry Ridgeway to Brompton	2½
(Churchstoke to the east 1½ miles via B4385)	
Brompton to Montgomery via Lymore	3¼
Total	11¼

Excluding return from Newcastle and diversion to Montgomery 9¾

Apart from the diversion to Montgomery this section follows the official route.

The ODP continues its northward progress crossing the eastern
edge of the Clun Forest which like nearby Kerry has given its name
to a breed of sheep. The area is intersected by a tangle of narrow
winding lanes, hugging the river courses where they can, but
obliged to escape them by steep climbs out of the narrow valleys.

Newcastle and the upper Clun valley from the ODP

Dyke and path which keep close company for most of the way take little account of such matters and head relentlessly northwards in a consistent if not always ruler straight line. The 5-mile dip and rise to the ancient Kerry Ridgeway provides the scenic pleasure expected from the ODP, but it is the northward prospect from just below the summit that may remain with the walker as the most cherished memory of the entire 180 miles.

The remaining 6 miles from the Kerry Ridgeway are downhill or level walking all the way to Montgomery.

NEWCASTLE TO HERGAN

The ODP crosses the road that runs north of the Clun Valley about ¹/₂ mile to the east of Newcastle and is found a short distance beyond Quarry House.

The retrospective view over the valley from the road and to the west as the ODP climbs the hillside presents a delightful picture. Trees chart the course of the dyke as it rolls in a gentle curve down to Lower Spoad with farm houses dotted amongst the green pasture.

The river makes a tortuous progress through the valley bottom in innumerable small contortions with the most agonised of the writhings between Bryndrinog and Clun's ancient bridge. Newcastle, seen from the hillside the top of the yellow flamed gorse, is at the junction of four roads and two rivers. The long broken lines of trees that mark out the field boundaries are sometimes seen to dramatic effect as they march darkly on the skyline.

As further height is gained an overall view of the steep hills and narrow valleys demonstrates what a difficult country this was to conquer and hold: every patch of woodland capable of hiding a guerrilla band, distant barns stabling for their horses, the dead ground behind every hillock a hiding place and a friend in every village to bring word of an advancing army bent on retribution. It is little wonder that men of the capabilities of Glyndwr, Llewelyn and the legendary Edric Sauvage were so difficult to pin down.

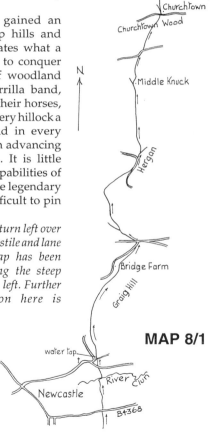

From the Newcastle road turn left over a stile to cross a short field to a stile and lane where a drinking water tap has been provided. Continue climbing the steep hillside with the dyke to your left. Further detailed route description here is superfluous, simply keep to the line of the dyke as it makes a gentle ellipse along the western flanks of Graig Hill, initially with some steep rises.

MAP 8/1

On the northern side of Graig Hill the ODP descends to cross a track to the east of Bridge Farm.

The ODP curves very gently to the right passing a pool seen below on the left and on to cross a stream about ¹/₄ mile north-east of the farm. Beyond the stream bear left soon to meet the road.

Turn right along the road to meet a junction where turn left and in a few yards right on a metalled lane passing newly restored cottages.

Just beyond a metal gate leave the track, forward slightly right, to climb through woodland with the dyke. As the wood falls back continue with the dyke, the encroaching gorse threatening the barelegged walker. Wispy strands of wool mark successful captures from passing sheep which nesting birds will in turn filch to line their nests.

The ODP descends a little with the ditch to your left to cross a short field to a stile to climb steeply through trees. The way curves to meet a stile where bear left for a few paces then swing right along the dyke with a period of level walking which leads to a broadening track to join the road under Hergan Hill.

HERGAN TO CHURCHTOWN

Cross the road and go forward on a track for a short distance. In about 30 yards bear diagonally left descending with the dyke to follow the fence line on your left. After crossing a stile bearing a Wild Edrics Way disc go ahead and in about 80 yards turn left over a stile and then sharp right keeping the boundary and the dyke to your right. (Note some maps may show the path following the eastern side of the fence.)

WILD EDRIC

Wild Edric is not as may be suspected some half crazed walker but a local Shropshire hero. He was to this border country what Hereward the Wake was to the fens of East Anglia. Many strange legends, with a familiar ring it must be said, have been attached to this Saxon landowner. They include a "Drakes Drum" myth that he will appear when the country is threatened by an enemy (he has of course been seen when war was impending), that he still gallops over the hills at a reckless pace at the head of his followers and that he haunts the ancient mines of the Stiperstones area. This is not the final catalogue of the unlikely stories which have veiled his memory in a cloak of myth and superstition. Another tradition associates him with the timeless fantasy that bewitched by siren music he was drawn to a house filled with beautiful young women. He takes one of their number to be his wife but she is no ordinary mortal and warns Edric that he must never question her absences from the marital home. Human nature being what it is there came the time when Edric failed to obey this injunction. Perhaps fuelled by a not unnatural jealous suspicion he determined to unravel the mystery and demands that she account for the time spent away. In so doing he has broken the unwritten marriage contract and pays the penalty with her immediate disappearance.

This wealth of impossible folklore which surrounds just one man does at least serve to illustrate the powerful reputation which he had built up locally. The reality is that Edric Sauvage, for that is his real name, bitterly resenting the Norman Conquest, gathered to him a like minded band of warriors and waged a not unsuccessful guerrilla war against them in the middle marches.

THE WALK CONTINUED

Maintain your northward direction over a succession of fields, keeping the fence line to your right throughout and dipping down to cross a small stream before climbing again to Middle Knuck reached in a little under ³/₄ mile after leaving Hergan.

Pass the barns of Middle Knuck to your right (the farm is now the Corve Dale Crisis Intervention Centre), shortly to meet and cross a stile. Cross the farm lane and continue, soon descending to a trickle of a stream. Climb again still with the dyke and fence to your right. The dyke as will have been noted elsewhere is lined with larch trees. At the top of the rise cross a stile and go forward a few paces to meet a road on a hill top that gives some fine views particularly to the east.

Turn half right onto the lane and then immediately left over a stile to continue with the dyke to your right. At the end of the field cross a stile and descend steeply through woodland.

CHURCHTOWN

As the plantation is left behind a surprise view is unveiled. This is Churchtown, set in a narrow valley hemmed in by the hills. Town is a considerable exaggeration for from here there is but a single house in sight, although the church could comfortably accommodate the needs of a fair sized village. This is St John the Baptist, a long narrow church with two bells hung in the smallest of towers and a

Surprise view to Churchtown

well kept churchyard. Within, a board announces its first rector as Morris ap Hugh appointed in 1572. Clearly the parish covers a wide rural area on both sides of the border with the inevitably decreasing population, but the church is in excellent order. There is a rather unusual piece of church furnishing, a large irregular stone placed
118

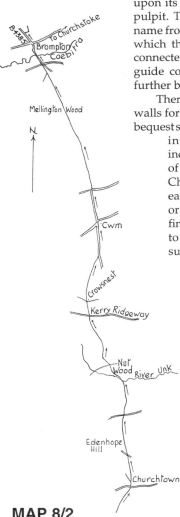

MAP 8/2

upon its own small carpet in front of the pulpit. The village of Mainstone gets its name from some linguistic tautology with which the stone may be assumed to be connected, the small but interesting church guide confirms this and provides some further background.

There are tables of benefactions on the walls for the period 1641 to 1728 with one bequest specifically for the very poor. Some intricate woodwork design is incorporated in the roof. The village of Mainstone, scarcely larger than Churchtown, is found $^{3}/_{4}$ mile to the east, those exploring the area by car or cycle may particularly enjoy the fine woodland above the village seen to its best when lit by the late spring sun.

This, and not the quartet of villages of the Clun valley is my candidate for the quietest place under the sun. Indeed it is so quiet that although I have scanned through Housman's often gloomy pages it appears that even his wandering feet and poet's eye somehow missed this corner of Shropshire.

CHURCHTOWN TO KERRY RIDGEWAY

From this surprise viewpoint bear half right down the hillside to cross the stream, a tributary of the oddly named

119

Descending the dyke to the Edenhope Valley and Nut Wood

River Unk, and meet the road a little to the left of the church.

Cross the road to a stile and gate and on to a further stile to follow the dyke which climbs steeply up the bracken and gorse covered hillside. The path is now well worn by the boots of earlier travellers so that their footfall on the narrow way has contrived to provide rough steps: useful at present but in danger of unsightly erosion as traffic along the dyke increases.

When a farm track is reached bear left for a few yards then over a stile and immediately right to resume your northern progress along the dyke. As you cross Edenhope Hill, there is an eastward view to the Long Mynd, Titterstone Clee and Brown Clee Hills and in the north-west the distant mountains of the Bala area.

Beyond the summit the ODP falls gently to meet and cross a road, here turn right and in a few steps left over a stile to descend with the dyke to the Edenhope Valley with the fence line to your right and a deep cleft to your left. Still on the route favoured by modern day followers of Wild Edric. Cross the stream, the infant Unk, in the valley bottom by stepping stones and turn left on a rising farm track.

In about 100 yards turn right over a stile into Nut Wood and bear half left up the hillside, following the line of the dyke. (Ignore grassy crossing track when met.) On leaving the trees maintain your northward direction initially with a fence on your right, soon walking along the top of the dyke with further fine views.

Beyond Nut Wood the dyke continues to meet the Kerry Ridgeway a

ODP by the Kerry Ridgeway

little beyond a gorse fringed pond where wild duck nest, an excellent refreshment stop.

THE KERRY RIDGEWAY

The Kerry Ridgeway has been called Wales' oldest road; it follows the crest of the hills above the Vale of Kerry for more than 15 miles from Cider House on the B4365 a few miles south of Newtown to Bishops Castle. For part of its course it serves as the boundary between England and Wales. As the ODP bisects the old road it passes from Shropshire into Powys and in 2 miles as the Caebitra is crossed, back into Shropshire. In less than a mile Offa's Dyke provides the modern boundary between the two counties. The route has been in use for at least 4,000 years, bronze age traders came this way and for 800 years the Welsh drovers brought herds of cattle and flocks of sheep along the ridge on the way to the English markets. Although several rivers rise close to the summit of the ridge water might well have been a problem and it is a matter of speculation whether the pond just south of the ridgeway was a natural waterhole or created to serve the needs of the drovers. Its western end is still only a track but from Pantglas it becomes a metalled, albeit narrow road.

THE ODP CONTINUED

From the pond a short gorse covered area is crossed to reach the Ridgeway, metalled at this point. Bishops Castle nearly 4 miles to the east, was from 1249 to 1967 the smallest borough in England, but rather too far off our route to make a diversion practical. It is a pleasant little town with several old inns and noted in the guides for its House on Crutches, a half timbered building with a considerable overhang supported in the manner suggested by its popular name.

Beyond the road descend by a track then over a stile on your right, to bear left to follow the dyke with views that improve as the woodland to the right falls back to allow a widening arc.

Before you the land falls away to the fields of Montgomery and Shropshire, a well watered promised land, lush green but as always it is the hills that command the attention. In the north-east the high wild spiny backed Stiperstones ridge is seen with the Devil's Chair

MAP 8/3

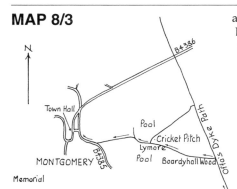

and Manstone Rock. Beyond the village of Church Stoke, where the large car park of Harry Tuffin's supermarket makes a white splash amongst the fields, rises Todleth Hill and the 1,683 feet high Corndon Hill which will be in sight for the next few miles. To the north the dark grey horizon is

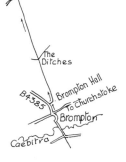

formed by the Berwyns, as the eye turns to the west the peaks of Arran Benyllyun and Arran Mawddwy make their mark and then the great bulk of Cader Idris.

The dyke falls steeply to meet a lane where turn left to reach the tiny black and white hamlet of Cwm in ¼ mile. Here the chapel, rebuilt in 1897, is now the Dyke Gallery.

Beyond the small green "roundabout" go ahead on the quiet lane. The steep bank to the right is one of nature's own wild gardens with dozens of species of wild flowers. One May day our list of finds included bluebells, primrose, vetch, yellow archangel, pink campion, greater and lesser stitchwort, cuckoo pint (otherwise known as lords and ladies), early purple orchid, wild strawberry, herb robert, wood anemone, digitalis (fox glove), shining cranesbill, speedwell and deadnettle.

In ¼ mile as the lane turns sharp right cross a stile and go forward with the dyke and hedge to your left. The ODP continues passing a caravan site on your right and making a delightful passage on the dyke through Mellington Wood.

Leave the woodland at a stile and go ahead with the hedgeline to your left and soon following the dyke as it becomes more obvious. At the end of the field pass through a further stretch of woodland, over a stile and bearing half right to meet a metalled lane where turn left and after passing under the archway of the lodge gates of Mellington Hall meet the road (B4385).

Go forward briefly returning to Shropshire as you cross the Caebitra by Brompton Bridge with a fine brick farm house (possibly a former mill) to your right.

At the next crossroads, the A489, Church Stoke is signed right, $1^1/_2$ miles, with shops, accommodation and a large Sunday market.

Continue with the B4385, signed Montgomery, for about 100 yards then turn right into the farm lane. Just short of the gateway to Brompton Hall (appropriately I noted some fine Brompton Stocks in the garden) turn left over a stile and follow the field edge with fence and dyke to your right. Maintain your direction to reach the white house known as The Ditches, presumably taking its name from the dyke.

Go through the gateway and over the drive to a metal gate and then through a short paddock with the house to your right. Continue along the field edge with the path following the dyke top at the end of the field.

Continue to cross a road and go ahead over further fields to meet a bridleway in $^3/_4$ mile.

Those continuing with the ODP should turn right over a cattle grid and then immediately left along field edge and woodland.

DIVERSION TO MONTGOMERY

Turn left along the metalled bridleway, soon to pass through Boardyhall Wood and the parkland of Lymore with some fine trees, notably copper beech. The bridleway passes between the upper and lower pools. Shortly after curving right past a barn take the bridleway on the left which leads to the road at the southern edge of Montgomery. Turn right soon to reach the town centre. (The tall pillar which you may have noted on the hillside to the south of Montgomery is the county war memorial.)

9: Over the Long Mountain
Montgomery to Welshpool

MAPS: 1:25,000 Pathfinder   909 (SO 29/39)
                                     888 (SJ 20/30)

            1:50,000 Landranger   137 Ludlow & Wenlock Edge
                                     126 Shrewsbury

FACILITIES: Shops, refreshments and accommodation at Montgomery and Welshpool with Bed and Breakfast signed on route near Forden and Buttington View.

PARKING FOR ROUND WALKS: Car parks and picnic sites, southern edge of Montgomery and at Buttington Wharf. (See also information in text on towpath walking.) Large car park in centre of Welshpool by Gateway Supermarket.

MILEAGE CHART:

Montgomery back to ODP	1$\frac{1}{4}$
ODP to Pound House	2$\frac{1}{2}$
Pound House to Nant Cribba (for Forden)	1
Nant Cribba to Beacon Ring	4$\frac{1}{4}$
Beacon Ring to Buttington Bridge	3
To Welshpool via the canal (not on the ODP)	2
Total	14
Official route	10$\frac{3}{4}$

With the exception of the link paths to Montgomery and Welshpool this section keeps to the official route.

Offa's Dyke continues over the fields to the east of Montgomery to Pound House providing a long stretch of almost level walking with the dyke at varying height. The dyke almost disappears as the ODP ascends a quarried hillside but soon returns with the dyke edging closer to the road at Nantcribba. The ODP follows the road with the dyke regained as it passes through the Kingswood area from whence it runs in parallel for a while with the Roman Road over the Long Mountain. ODP and the dyke enter Leighton Woods but take

Montgomery Town Hall

divergent courses as the ODP makes for higher ground to be briefly reunited near Buttington. The route is a mix of field paths, quiet lanes, and woodland providing views over the valley of the Severn with the connection to Welshpool made by the Montgomery Canal, now part of a larger network known as the Shropshire Union.

MONTGOMERY

Time has laid a gentle hand on Montgomery, so much so that you could believe that the clock stopped ticking 200 years ago. Turning into the aptly named Broad Street where its once important market was held you look up the street to the impressively large brick built Georgian Town Hall, a symbol of past prosperity. Take away the parked cars, remove the tarmac from the centre of the street and you have a ready made set that would delight any film director and enchant his lighting cameraman.

Daniel Defoe was not quite so taken with Montgomery, after recording that it was a great frontier town in the border wars he goes on to say (around 1725) that he found it much decayed. Happily it's fortunes were set to improve.

The town, and the former county, owes its name or more correctly its English name to a Norman, Roger de Montgomery. Roger, a kinsman of William, Duke of Normandy, actively encouraged the invasion of Britain providing a fleet of sixty ships and playing an important role in his victory at Hastings in 1066, the most memorable date in English history. The first battle was won but what lay ahead was to prove far more difficult, far more costly, the subjucation of England and in particular Wales and the border country. It was a task that was to occupy William and his successors for many a long and bloody year.

Roger was rewarded with his appointment as the Earl of Shrewsbury. No sinecure this, for he was charged with the care of troubled territory and immediately engaged in the construction of a series of castles including the first of the Montgomery fortresses. This was located to the north-west of the present town at Hen Domen not far from the site of a Roman Fort. Not that the Romans were first to build in the area for the early iron age Britons had occupied a site at Ffridd Faldwyn which had been in use since Neolithic times.

The continuing border troubles demanded the construction of a second castle by Baldwin de Boller which gave the town its Welsh name Trefaldwyn - Baldwins Town. In 1223 a third castle was built on the orders of Henry III on the high cliff overlooking the town that was to grow beneath its protective shadow. Today only scant ruins remain but the views are superb. In the eastern arc are the now familiar Corndon Hill, the Stiperstones and the Long Mynd, to the south the Kerry Ridgeway and in the north the Berwyns and the Long Mountain.

The town is proud of its long history and a large and enthusiastic team of volunteers man the museum, The Old Bell, close to the Town Hall in Arthur Street. A visit is recommended (for opening times see the Useful Information section). The exhibits include the story of the Forden House of Industry, built in 1792 under the poor laws to accommodate some 500 people. The regime must have been a strict one for its equipment included a bridle for scolds, a straight jacket for the punishment of the unruly and in 1795 the authorities found it necessary to provide two pairs of stocks.

More of Montgomery's history is told on plaques placed on a

number of buildings. One records that in 1840 the town was able to support over 50 tradesmen, among them 2 blacksmiths, 5 bakers, 3 bootmakers, 3 carpenters, 8 grocers, 4 drapers and coopers, maltsters, plumbers, masons, saddlers, a timber merchant and a tanner. Clearly an improvement on the situation described by Defoe 85 years earlier. The Town Hall clock of 1921 commemorates a remarkable and perhaps unique civic achievement by Alderman Nicholas Watson Fairles-Humphrey who was mayor on no less than fifteen occasions.

The castle was for long the home of the Herbert family one of whose number, Sir Richard Herbert, has a magnificent canopied and coloured tomb in St Nicholas church. Richard is shown neatly bearded, arrayed in armour with a dog at his feet. Beside him lies the effigy of his wife although having married again she is buried elsewhere. Around them in dutiful attendance are their children, six sons and two daughters.

Beneath the splendid attire and grandeur of the tomb lies the reality of mortal men with the representation of two corpses clad in the last dress of death, simple shrouds. Sir Richard was Member of Parliament for Montgomery in 1585 and his brother George was the poet and Latin scholar. Their father, Sir Edward Herbert was much involved in keeping the peace in Wales as Deputy Constable of Aberystwyth Castle and later as Sheriff of Montgomery and Member of Parliament.

Other items of interest in the church include the well preserved and quite magnificent Royal Coat of Arms of George I dated 1726, and two effigies set in the floor, one of which is thought to represent Sir Edmund Mortimer. Mortimer's story has been related earlier in this book (chapter 6); he died you may remember from starvation during the siege of Harlech castle in 1409. At the back of the church is a monument to a distinguished naval officer, Sir Charles Thomas Jones, rear admiral of the blue, who took part in the capture of Toulon in 1783, the action of the "Glorious First of June" in 1784 and later held command of an 18 gun warship in the West Indies. A quite extraordinarily large "benefaction table" measuring 8 by 6 feet bearing the Herbert coat of arms records the restoration of the tower at the expense of the Rt Hon Edward Herbert, Viscount Clive and Lymore. A larger proclamation of an act of charity I have yet to see

The Clun Valley and Graig Hill, Newcastle
Crossing the River Unk

Clun bridge

Right:
Llanymynech quarries

in a church.

In the churchyard a disputed verdict is still remembered at the Robbers Grave, now marked by a holly and rose bush. It recalls the sad story of John Newton Davies who was hanged as a highwayman in 1821. Throughout Davies protested his innocence but to no avail. In desperation he pleaded that after his death the court of heaven would demonstrate his innocence by an omen - that the grass would never grow upon his grave. It seems for many years that his grave was indeed bare of grass although patently that is not the case today.

Montgomery Castle was slighted after the English Civil War but its part in the conflict is intertwined with the story of Sir Thomas Myddleton of Chirk and must be left for the moment.

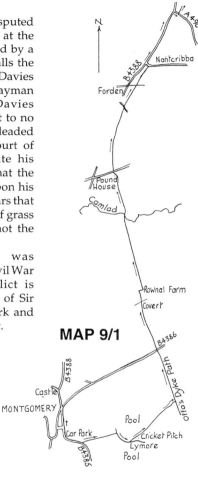

MAP 9/1

MONTGOMERY

RETURN TO THE ODP

From the Town Hall walk down Broad Street and turn right on the B4385 to follow this to the edge of the town, where take the bridleway on the left found just beyond the car park and picnic site. Follow this eastwards over the fields for just over ¼ mile to turn right on the bridleway that passes through Lymore Park. In about 250 yards take the signed path on the left, not a right of way but a permissive path, which crosses fields with the cricket pitch away to your right. The house at Lymore was demolished earlier this century and the path you are following seems to be a recent introduction since it does not appear on my OS maps at time of writing, but is a useful shortcut back to the ODP.

The path meets a waymarked stile on the outside edge of a wooded area, ignore the left fork and go ahead over an open field with woodland to your right to cross a further waymarked stile. Bear right along the hedgeline to meet and join the ODP by a stile. Do not cross the stile but turn to follow the ODP, a little north of west, keeping the hedgeline to your right.

ODP TO POUND HOUSE

The dyke here forms the boundary between England and Wales. At the end of the first field cross a stile to continue on the dyke with the extra elevation providing a view to Montgomery and the encircling hills which enclose the wide lowland basin.

Half a mile after rejoining the ODP the B4386 is met and crossed. You are, briefly, back in England, with the small village of Chirbury nearly 2 miles to your right. From the road pass through a gateway and maintain your direction with field boundaries and Rownal Covert to your right. At the end of the field beyond the covert turn right over a stile and immediately left on the dyke to reach and turn right on the track to Rownal Farm.

Cross a stile on the left as you reach the house and follow the hedgeline (to your right) with the dyke a little way to the left. At the bottom of the field pass through a gateway to follow an old hedged lane for ¼ mile or so, passing derelict cottages separated by a dried up pool with the second cottage with its wellhead pump seen close to the ODP. This is almost a secret path which eventually opens out beyond a metal gateway to cross a small stream by a stone slab bridge.

The route of the ODP which used to head north-west to Salt Bridge was diverted in 1988 and is now waymarked forward to meet and cross a fast flowing little stream by a bridge - "Built by the Powis Task Force -07- Knighton 1985". Thank you gentlemen, an excellent job.

The stream is the Camlad, unique in being the only river to rise in England and flow into Wales, but the benefit of its water which is surely not in short supply in Wales, is soon returned for the Camlad flows on to contribute its resources to the Severn.

Beyond the bridge bear half left to follow the field boundary and part way down the field cross the stile found on your right and turn left on a track which continues to the road passing Pound House to your left. (Note the owl boxes set in the trees.)

The dyke actually passes under the house which was built in 1820. Since it is a remote location away from any village pound for stray animals it may be assumed that the enclosure from which it took its name was used as an overnight stop or collecting point by the drovers.

POUND HOUSE TO NANTCRIBBA

Cross the road to a stile opposite and over a very short field to a further stile and stream bearing up the field boundary to meet and cross a stile, on the right, in about 100 yards and enter a lightly wooded area. Bear half left up the steep hillside to leave this former quarry by a stile and go forward with a hedge and dyke to your right.

At end of the field cross a stile, now with the dyke more prominent, and turn right over a stile and then left to maintain your direction with the dyke and hedge to your left. Views to your right include Corndon Hill. Continue with the line of trees along the dyke descending a little to a stile at the end

of the field. Cross a short field with a corrugated iron barn to your right to meet and cross a lane. (Bed and Breakfast sign here - Railway Inn ½ mile.)

Beyond the lane go ahead, gently rising with views to Corndon Hill and the Stiperstones and continue with the dyke over fields passing Parklands and a pond to your right. Keep with the field boundary, crossing a stile to meet the lane to Nantcribba (site of

Trees line the dyke near Forden

131

castle). Turn left to meet the road, B4388 and turn right. (Those intending to visit Forden should turn left.)

NANTCRIBBA TO BEACON RING

Follow the road for ½ mile to meet and turn right on the A490 (signed Churchstoke). In 60 yards turn left in front of a house and cross a stile to pass through a fenced area and over a further stile keeping the farm buildings on the left. Thence over a short field to a stile and continue with the field boundary to your left. Maintain your direction over further fields to meet a lane at the little hamlet of Kingswood. A notice at either end of the last field reads "The strings are to stop the hens flying over the stile, please replace." At the lane turn left and then almost immediately right up a gravelled path which is soon left to follow a path between trees and a hedge to cross a stile. Keep the same line of travel over a short field with a hedge and house to your left following the dyke. Continue over a further field to a stile by a wooden outhouse to meet a lane and go forward, ie. half right, on this.

The lane follows the course of the Roman road that climbed over the Long Mountain, the dyke builders opted for the same line and it will be seen beyond the hedge first on your right then on the left.

Keep with the rising lane for ½ mile passing the Georgian style Court House to your right. The occasional gateway on the left gives brief glimpses of the valley of the Severn with the distant Powis Castle, sometimes called the red castle, glowing pink through the greenery.

As the road swings to the right leave it to turn left through the gateway of Greenwood Lodge. Bear right passing the house to take the broad track which climbs steadily through woodland - larch and other conifers with some broadleaf. The ODP route through the woodland is very well waymarked. Here and there the track is lined with rosebay willow-herb, more colourfully called fireweed, rhododendrons and even a flowering raspberry cane - perhaps the accidental end product of some marauding bird's visit to a local garden.

It is a long pull up the hillside, shut in by the banked forest to your right and with only a veiled view to your left. As the track levels out, bear right over a crossing path to continue on a broad forest road. Monkey Puzzle trees make an appearance in the woodland scene with no view save a narrow band of sky and perhaps the sight of soaring buzzards who nest in the vicinity.

MP 9/2

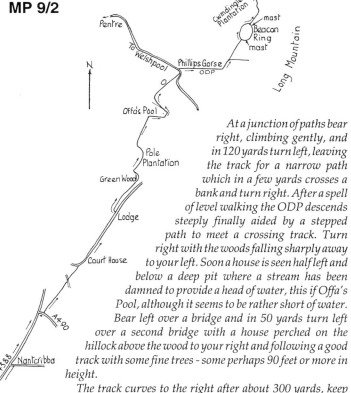

At a junction of paths bear right, climbing gently, and in 120 yards turn left, leaving the track for a narrow path which in a few yards crosses a bank and turn right. After a spell of level walking the ODP descends steeply finally aided by a stepped path to meet a crossing track. Turn right with the woods falling sharply away to your left. Soon a house is seen half left and below a deep pit where a stream has been damned to provide a head of water, this if Offa's Pool, although it seems to be rather short of water. Bear left over a bridge and in 50 yards turn left over a second bridge with a house perched on the hillock above the wood to your right and following a good track with some fine trees - some perhaps 90 feet or more in height.

The track curves to the right after about 300 yards, keep with it until a further and much better endowed pool is reached. Leave the track here as it bears left, to continue forward keeping the tree fringed pool to your left. The path follows the inside edge of the wood with the farm buildings of Pant-y-Bwch seen on the hill half left. On meeting a lane turn left and in about 200 yards turn right.

At this point there is a view to Welshpool spread out to the north of the Severn. (Travellers overtaken by bad weather or failing light may opt to head to the town more directly. Ignore the turn just mentioned and keep to the lane via Pentre to turn right on the B4388

then left on the B4381, over the
Severn by Leighton Bridge and
thence to Welshpool - about 2½
miles.)

*To continue with the ODP follow
the lane which climbs steadily, at*

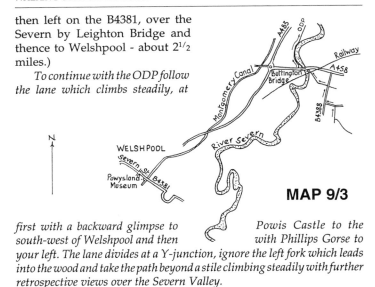

MAP 9/3

first with a backward glimpse to   *Powis Castle to the*
south-west of Welshpool and then   *with Phillips Gorse to*
*your left. The lane divides at a Y-junction, ignore the left fork which leads
into the wood and take the path beyond a stile climbing steadily with further
retrospective views over the Severn Valley.*

*At the top of the field turn left over a stile and go forward along the edge
of Phillips Gorse to cross a stile in about 100 yards. Follow the field
boundary (on your right). At the top of the field cross a stile on your right
and turn left to follow the fence line towards the wooded Beacon Ring with
a wireless mast seen ahead.*

The egg shaped "ring" now much obscured by dense woodland
is an ancient hill-fort on the 1,338 feet summit of the Long Mountain.
Within the ring a stone with many of its leaded letters missing
records the tree planting in December 1953 - coincidental with
coronation year with which a connection might be assumed, tree
plantings being a popular commemorative activity at the time.

BEACON RING TO BUTTINGTON BRIDGE

*Once in the ring bear left to follow the gorse covered banks on the western
side of the earthworks providing views to Welshpool and the river valley.
At the far end bear right to complete the half circle heading towards a
wireless mast and covered reservoir. Turn left over a stile and go ahead,
reservoir to your right, on a path that is in danger of becoming overgrown.*

The path emerges from the trees to meet a slightly wider track before continuing through the woodland. Ignore the first left turn and when the main track curves left keep with it but in 60 yards bear right on a narrow path to leave the forest.

Beyond the wood bear half left over fields now with one of the fine airy views that is such a rewarding feature of the Offa's Dyke Path, in this instance to the Severn Valley, the hill pastures broken by a darker forest green. Part way over the field a marker post directs you slightly diagonally

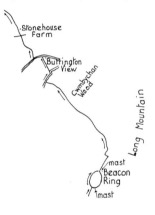

left to the top corner of the field to cross a stile by a metal gate. Follow the fence line over a short stretch of field to a gateway and stile. From here it is downhill all the way. Descend with the fenceline.

Welshpool is back in sight, to your right the Breidden Hills topped by Rodneys Pillar, a glimpse of the Severn and the broadening valley as the river flows on to meet the English border.

At the end of the field, cross a stile and bear half right over a falling field with improving views of river, road and rail in the valley from which a scatter of farms climb the hillsides.

Beyond the stile continue the descent with the field boundary to your right. At the foot of the field meet a gateway and stile and turn right on a quiet lane. In about 200 yards after some tortuous turns cross a stile on your left and descend over a large field to a stile and go ahead with hedge to your left to meet a lane.

Turn left and follow the lane for 200 yards to meet a stile on your right which also carries a Glyndwrs Way sign.

Bear diagonally right over the field towards a clump of trees, where turn sharp left to meet and follow field boundary, on your left, to a stile. Beyond the stile turn right along a rutted track to a gateway and stile by a house from which bear right along the lane to pass Stonehouse Farm to your right.

At the end of the barns bear half right over a short field to a stile set midway up the hedgeline beyond which is a farm track. Leave the track after only a short distance to go half left over the field to a stile and gate at the far corner. Continue with a small stream to your right; about three quarters of the way down the field cross a stile and stone bridge and bear half left over the field to a stile in the opposite corner. Head slightly diagonally left passing under power lines to a stile and turn left on a wider track to meet and turn right on the road, the B4388.

Offa's Dyke Business Park on your right signals your return to the modern age. As the first of some chalet bungalows is approached turn left over a short field to cross a stream by a plank bridge then a further field and plank bridge and continue to a white stile to cross the (working) railway line.

The road, A458 is met beyond the next field, where turn left to cross the Severn by Buttington Bridge. A very different river from the tidal waters of the estuary seen from the start of the ODP.

The Anglo-Saxon Chronicle records that Buttington was the scene of a great battle between the Danes and Saxons in AD894. Clearly this has long been an important crossing of the Severn, not so very far from the present border and one of the gateways to Wales.

If not visiting Welshpool, turn right with the signed ODP just beyond the bridge, the route is described in the next chapter.

BUTTINGTON BRIDGE TO WELSHPOOL

Welshpool bound walkers should continue with the road to the roundabout and take the road signed Buttington Wharf to join the Montgomery Canal - shown on maps as The Shropshire Union Canal. An information board describes the canal, currently under restoration, as "a museum of early nineteenth century transport". The towpath provides some excellent walking and more of it will be explored in the next day's itinerary.

Turn left under the canal bridge and follow the quiet waterway to reach Welshpool in 2 miles. The canal has to be left briefly to cross the road due to the lack of a suitable bridge - one of the problems to be resolved as the restoration work progresses. As the Powysland Museum is reached leave the canal to turn right up Severn Street to the town centre with shops, including some mouthwatering butchers and bakers, and accommodation.

10: Waterside Walking
Welshpool to Llanymynech

MAPS: 1:25,000 Pathfinder   888 (SJ 20/30)
                                    868 (SJ 21/31)
                                    847 (SJ 22/32)

         1:50,000 Landranger   126 Shrewsbury

FACILITIES: Shops, refreshments and accommodation at Welshpool and
    Llanymynech. Accommodation possibilities on or near route at Pool
    Quay.

PARKING FOR ROUND WALKS: Central car park, Welshpool, Buttington
    Wharf and behind Dolphin Inn, Llanymynech - all these useful for
    towpath walking.

MILEAGE CHART:

Welshpool to return to ODP Buttington Bridge	2
Buttington Bridge to Pool Quay	2
Pool Quay to Four Crosses	5$^{1}/_{2}$
Four Crosses to Llanymynech via towpath	2$^{3}/_{4}$
Total	12$^{1}/_{4}$
Total via ODP only	10$^{1}/_{4}$

Apart from the link from Welshpool this section follows the official route.

This section is level walking with three visits to the quiet towpath
of the Montgomery Canal and two passages along the River Severn.
Pleasant if not exciting walking and those whose schedule is
becoming tight may consider this is a section that might be skipped
or the time used to visit Powis Castle. There is a bus link between
Welshpool and Llanymynech - a timetable check is recommended
- see Useful Information section.

Offa's Dyke is not met again for some miles its place taken by the
much later earthworks of the Severn floodbanks. It reappears
shortly after the crossing of the Derwas Bridge over the New Cut.

The former Cambrian Railway bisected the dyke at Four Crosses, beyond which the dyke follows the alignment of the present day A483 northwards towards Llanymynech. The ODP which originally took the same route now forsakes the road at Llandysilio for the final sampling of the attractive towpath of the Montgomery Canal.

WELSHPOOL

Welshpool is a busy market town in the Severn Valley, a few miles from the border with England. Happily it has not been overwhelmed by the standardised façades of the national retail chains and can still rejoice in some highly individual shops. The leading attraction for the tourist is Powis Castle, in medieval times the home of the Princes of Powys and later of the Herbert family, today it is one of the finest jewels of the National Trust.

Welshpool has other stories to tell, the Powysland Museum and Canal Centre now attractively housed in a restored warehouse. The museum grew from the work of a local history society, the Powysland Club founded in 1867. The centre presents the history of the locality from Neolithic times to the present century, with particular emphasis on local trades, farming of course, coopering and hatting, one of the

towns mainstays in the eighteenth and early nineteenth century. In a section devoted to money there is an ear trumpet, formerly part of the equipment of the local Becks Bank, not apparently for the convenience of the hard of hearing but used before the days of pass books and bank statements to

The beginning of a dynasty? Plaque on a Welshpool building commemorating the first Welsh Jones

communicate in whispers to customers at the counter the state of their account. Admission is free and as the museum is by the canal in Severn Street a visit may be included as part of the onward journey.

The most common name in Wales must surely be Jones but who was the original patriarch of this great family? A plaque on a house at the top of Church Street suggests an explanation, it reads - "This house was erected in 1692 by Gilbert and Ann Jones whose ancestor Roger Jones, temp Edward VI, is reputed to have been the first Welsh Jones, and paid to the Lord of Powys the feudal due of a peppercorn at Midsummer. In the eighteenth century it was occupied by William Owen, saddler (1718-1759), grandfather and Robert Owen, saddler (1741-1804) father of Robert Owen (1771-1858) - the social reformer, founder of the co-operation and infant day schools...".

Robert Owen moved to Newtown a few miles to the west where his son, most of whose reforming work took place in Lanarkshire, is commemorated by a museum and memorial.

At the foot of the church steps is a half timbered house, originally called Magpie Cottage but now renamed in honour of Grace Evans, one of the participants in a classic escape story. The plot has all the essential elements of costume drama. Let the scene be set.

The year is 1716, the main characters, William Maxwell, 5th Earl of Nithsdale, his wife the Countess and George I, King of Great Britain and Ireland the first of the Hanoverian monarchs. It has been a time of unrest, particularly in Scotland where there is strong support for the return of "The Old Pretender", James Edward Stewart. In the autumn of 1715 the earl proclaimed his support for the English Jacobites and in November was given a command at the Battle of Preston. The town was under siege for two days before the Jacobites surrendered.

The curtain rises on Act Three. Scene 1. Nithsdale together with other rebels have been put on trial and condemned to death. Scene 2. A reprieve is granted to three of them but Nithsdale is not of that number and is due to be beheaded within the week. His distraught wife presents herself at court and implores the king to show mercy to her husband but to no avail. Scene 3. Time - the eve of the execution. Lady Nithsdale together with a group of friends including

Grace Evans go to the Tower of London. Incredibly, lax security or maybe it was collusion, allows the Earl to change into female clothing and leave the Tower in the company of the other ladies and make good his escape to France.

POWIS CASTLE

Powis Castle occupies a commanding position on the high ground to the west of the Severn with views over the valley to the Long Mountain. A strategic location not overlooked by builders of earlier motte and baileys close to the site of the present castle. The castle, once the home of the Princes of Powys, lives up to its Welsh name - Castell Coch - the red castle.

In the sixteenth century it came into the hands of the Herbert family whose descendents, the Earls of Powis, have cared for the castle until the present century when it was bequeathed to the National Trust. During the Civil War the castle was taken by the Parliamentarians during a hectic period of activity in the autumn of 1644 which dealt a heavy blow to Royalist prospects in this part of the border country. Happily the castle was spared the destructive punishment that was commonly meted out to those held to be "on the wrong side".

Powis Castle should not be missed, set in extensive parkland with terraced gardens on the same scale as the castle. Figures along the balustrade, a kilted piper and a shepherdess look out over further gardens which in turn give way to lawns and herbaceous borders bright with colour. Huge topiaried yews match the size of the castle and set off the giant wisteria which climbs the walls while secret arbors under clipped yews give vistas down garden paths.

In the castle courtyard a sculpture of Fame on a winged horse with bugle blowing sets the scene for the splendour of the house and in particular the collection of treasures assembled by Robert Clive - Clive of India.

Shropshire born Robert Clive started a long career in India with an appointment in the East Indian Company's service at Madras in 1743. In the following year England was at war with the French, Clive was taken prisoner but later released. In 1748 he exchanged pen for sword as he embarked upon a military career of such distinction that he became one of the great heroes of the eighteenth

Powys Castle. Welshpool

century. Government and the East India Company showered praises upon him. In 1762 he was created Baron Clive of Plassey and two years later made a Knight of the Bath. On his return to England he served as member of parliament for Shrewsbury but continuing problems in India led to his return to implement much needed reforms.

During his long career in the sub-continent Clive amassed a great fortune which in later years led to a parliamentary enquiry following accusations of corruption. The charges were never substantiated and appear out of character but nevertheless left the inevitable cloud over his outstanding achievements. It should be remembered that it was the custom for those serving in India in civil and military capacities to engage in trading on their own account. Such were the opportunities that many a family's fortune was founded beneath the skies of Bengal. Always something of a solitary man Clive was subject to fits of depression and his death from an overdose of opium taken to relieve stomach pains may have been

141

suicide: a sad end to a brilliant career at the early age of 49.

Beyond the Clive galleries the tour of the house continues, fine painted ceilings, rich tapestries, a magnificent staircase, panelled rooms, pictures and portraits - indeed all you might expect from a great house.

WELSHPOOL TO RETURN TO ODP AT BUTTINGTON BRIDGE

From the centre of the town head down Severn Street to reach the Montgomery Canal by the Powysland Museum, turn left and follow the towpath, briefly interrupted by a road crossing, as far as Buttington Wharf.

THE MONTGOMERY CANAL

The canal is the subject of a challenging restoration programme. Information boards at various points detail its history and the rich wildlife that may be found along its 35-mile length. So far as our itinerary is concerned these are located at Buttington Wharf, Carreghofa Locks and at the foot of the bridge at Llanymynech. When fully reopened the canal will offer some delightfully peaceful cruising but at the moment it is canoeists and walkers that most benefit. The towpath, although not a definitive right of way, is open for most of its length.

The work includes the restoration of dry sections a little beyond Llanymynech and at Frankton: a costly reconstruction of a number of modern bridges which at present leave the canal with little headroom for a water rat never mind a narrow boat. The canal linked Newtown, once famous for its Welsh flannel, with the Llangollen Canal at Frankton north-east of Oswestry. The construction of the canal by several different companies, began towards the end of the eighteenth century, but did not reach Newtown until 1819. Commercial considerations and the advent of the railway age brought mergers and the waterway became part of the Shropshire Union network.

BUTTINGTON BRIDGE TO POOL QUAY

You may if you wish continue with the canal but to rejoin the official route of the ODP leave it at Buttington Wharf and take the road to the roundabout and continue eastwards with the A458 to Buttington Bridge.

MAP 10/1

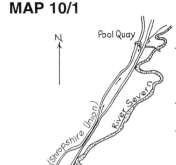

Do not cross the river, but turn left on a track soon passing a white house on your left. The Severn with its seemingly fragile earthen banks is followed for about 300 yards. Beyond the second stile as the river starts to curve away leave it to follow the floodbank over the fields. At a stile as the river returns to meet you continue ahead cutting off a further loop of the river and shortly resuming the path along the floodbank to meet the road, the A483. Turn right with the road and follow the vergeside path for nearly ½ mile.

The canal curves in to run in close company with the road on the left. On the right close to the Severn the map marks the site of Strata Marcella Abbey, but from the road there is not as much as a single stone to be seen. It was a Cistercian monastery founded in 1170 by Owain Cyfeiliog, a poet prince of Powys, who later in life took on the white monk's habit of the order. Giraldis in his *Journey through Wales* refers briefly to a scandal attached to the name of its first Abbot, Enoch, who was tempted into a short lived elopement with a nun.

At a slight rise in the road join the canal towpath to follow it north-westerly for ¾ mile.

Mile plates along the way also commemorate events and people, like the 21st year of the restoration work or those who have contributed to the project. The clear water reflects the soft green of the tree fringed waterway in contrast with the great rolling yellow carpet of headily scented oilseed rape which sweeps down the hillside. The towpath is lined with wild flowers, primroses, bugle, cuckoo pint, ramsons and marsh marigold.

A wicket gate leads into the lock area as you pass the whitewashed houses of Pool Quay to continue towards the first deep narrow lock. Just

143

short of the lock leave the towpath to join a lane and turn right, soon to meet the road. (Note pub to your right.)

POOL QUAY TO FOUR CROSSES.

In favourable circumstances the Severn was once navigable as far as Pool Quay with cargoes brought upstream in shallow draught boats hauled by teams of men. A hard life you might suppose but when the first towpaths were introduced further downstream to facilitate the use of horsepower there was much discontent at the threatened loss of livelihood.

Turn left with the road, ignore the first track seen on the right, and as the road rises by a barn turn right over a stile. Head diagonally left over a field to meet a stile, beyond which bear slightly right to meet a bridge to the left of a metal gateway. Continue to join the floodbank and on to cross one of the now disused lines of the Cambrian Railway.

The ODP continues along the floodbanks for nearly 3 miles, following a straighter, but by no means direct course, than that of the many twists and turns of the river.

Fine cattle graze the meadows, Fresians in milk, bullocks, and the occasional brown and white faced Hereford. Sharing the grassland are a handful of swans, while larks soar high above, their song interrupted by the occasional call of a curlew. Scenically the interest is concentrated on the Breidden Hills which rise sharply from the valley near Criggion. Breidden Hill, much quarried and volcanic in origin was long occupied with a hill fort dating from at least 750BC and there are traces of farming activities from a more distant time. From the ODP a tall column can be seen - Rodney's Pillar erected to commemorate the Admiral's victory over the French off Dominica in 1782. This isolated group of hills, a landmark seen from all points of the compass, provides an all round view. A walk to the summit is included in the author's *Severn Walks* also published by Cicerone.

Rising in competition with the hills are the tall masts of British Telecom's Criggion Radio Station. As you near the end of the masts beyond Red House continue along the bank with a lane seen to your left and passing Upper House. The bank curves away from the Severn to meet the sluice gates by the New Cut. A sharp change of direction here, as the cut is followed westwards for about 400 yards to meet and cross the Derwas

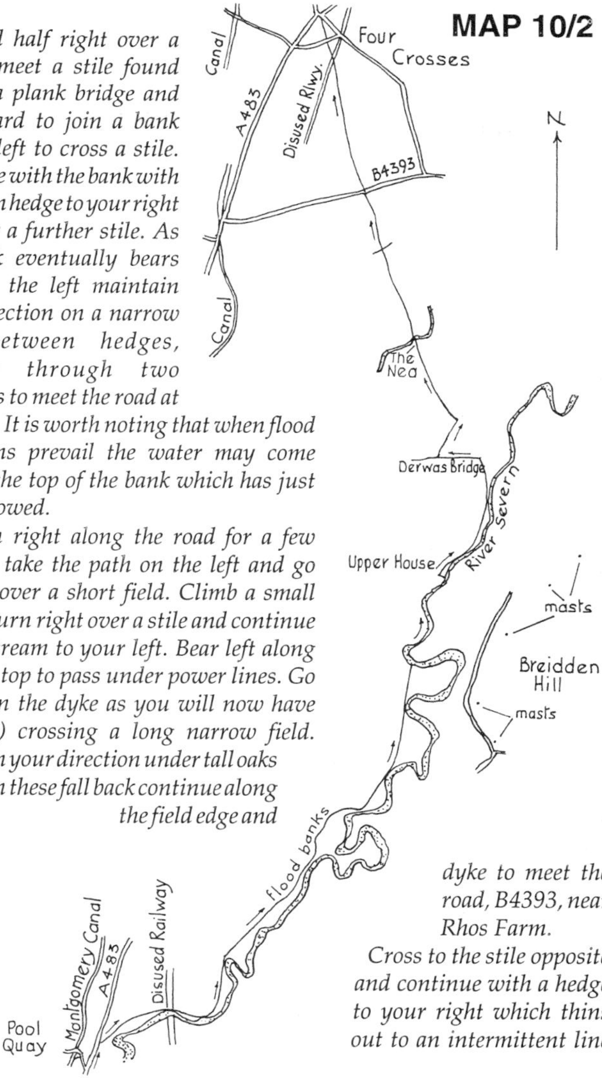

Bridge.

Head half right over a field to meet a stile found beyond a plank bridge and go forward to join a bank bearing left to cross a stile. Continue with the bank with hawthorn hedge to your right and over a further stile. As the bank eventually bears away to the left maintain your direction on a narrow path between hedges, passing through two gateways to meet the road at The Nea. It is worth noting that when flood conditions prevail the water may come close to the top of the bank which has just been followed.

Turn right along the road for a few yards to take the path on the left and go forward over a short field. Climb a small bank to turn right over a stile and continue with a stream to your left. Bear left along the bank top to pass under power lines. Go ahead (on the dyke as you will now have gathered) crossing a long narrow field. Maintain your direction under tall oaks and when these fall back continue along the field edge and

MAP 10/2

dyke to meet the road, B4393, near Rhos Farm.

Cross to the stile opposite and continue with a hedge to your right which thins out to an intermittent line

145

of trees. At the top of this large field cross a stile and go ahead now with the hedge to your left to reach Gornel Farm. Pass through the farmyard with the buildings to your right and follow the fence, to your left, to a gate and stile. Continue on a fenced path passing sprinkler beds to reach a gateway. Cross the small industrial estate at Four Crosses following the waymarking as indicated by the notice - ie. diagonally left to pass works buildings to your right to meet the road.

Cross the road to follow the dyke over a small field with a pond to your left to meet a further road, the B4393, close to the junction which seems to

MAP 10/3

have given the village its name rather than any religious connection.

Turn left then immediately right to follow the A483 signed Oswestry. Ahead will be seen the high cliff of the quarried southern face of Llanymynech Hill some 2 miles off. Keep with the road for ¼ mile passing the Golden Lion and the neat cream painted school with its single bell.

Turn left to follow Parsons Lane for ¼ mile to meet the Montgomery Canal (Shropshire Union on maps) by bridge 99. Turn right to follow the towpath for 2 miles to Llanymynech.

This is another delightful stretch of the canal constructed above the level of the land to the right where Charolais cattle may be seen in the fields. In ¾ mile a three arched aqueduct takes the canal over the River Vyrnwy which later forms the boundary between England and Wales before it makes its contribution to the Severn near Crew Green. The ironwork of the bridge is scarred by the tow ropes of horse drawn barges.

Beyond the bridge ignore the waymark which signs a path off right and continue with the towpath to meet and cross the road by yet another bridge which will need to be raised before the canal can be fully navigable.

Montgomery Canal - Carreghofa locks

The canal curves towards Carreghofa Locks where cottages, like bookends, are sited on each side of the bridge. Two locks at Carreghofa and a toll house mark the junction of the Montgomery Canal and the Llanymynech branch of the Ellesmere Canal. An information board gives further historical detail of the waterway and the rivalry between the two companies.

Continue with the towpath to reach Llanymynech Bridge in just under a mile, leaving the canal after passing under the A483 bridge.

11: The Quarry Way
Llanymynech to Oswestry

MAPS: 1:25,000 Pathfinder   847 (SJ 22/32)
           1:50,000 Landranger   126 Shrewsbury

FACILITIES: Shops, refreshments and accommodation at Llanymynech and Oswestry.

PARKING FOR ROUND WALKS: Llanymynech (behind Dolphin Inn), Old Racecourse picnic site Oswestry.

MILEAGE CHART:

Llanymynech to Nantmawr	$3^1/_4$
Nantmawr to the Morda Bridge and the Old Mill, Llanforda	3
Diversion to Oswestry	$2^1/_2$
Total	$8^3/_4$

Apart from the diversion to Oswestry this section follows the official route throughout.

This short section which might be accomplished during the course of a morning allows time for an afternoon's exploration of Oswestry. It follows pleasant undulating albeit much quarried countryside using field and woodland paths and quiet lanes. The quarrying activities seem to have destroyed sections of the dyke and the ODP diverts well to the west of its line. The dyke headed northwards to the foot of Llanymynech Hill from whence it made a westward curve along the slopes leaving the hill fort on the English side of the border. The ODP picks up the line of the dyke and continues with it as it skirts the golf course but leaves it to descend briefly to the valley whilst Offa's boundary follows Blodwel Rocks. The dyke which has dipped to the valley near Whitehaven makes the frontier on the western side of the Llynclys quarries and continues northwards via Treflach to Fron where it is reunited with the ODP.

LLANYMYNECH

Llanymynech lies on the very border between England and Wales, a border delineated by Offa's Dyke and the more modern arbiters of such matters, the Boundary Commission. In the ages between the

The much quarried Llanymynch Hill from Pen-y-foel

reality of the dividing line moved with the power of the sword rather than the stroke of a political quill, but such matters apart times have changed for Llanymynech perhaps as much in this century as any other. Turn back the clock eighty years or more to reveal a very different scene from the one the walker finds today...

A great plume of smoke curls high into the sky from the single chimney of the quarry works. Gangs of men perspire as they load coal to fire a long brick kiln. The sound of shot blasting echoes off the hillside to send the birds whirring into the air in a great commotion. Clouds of dust rise and settle to leave a white residue on the hedgerows and washing left out injudiciously. The screaming whine of the winch engine adds its song to the rhythmic bump and thump of sturdy tank engines shunting wagons about the spiders web of tracks. From the canal, its waters streaked by coal dust and coloured by the shot silk slicks of leaking oil, a dull percussive thud adds to the symphony of the industrial mayhem as barges moored in the little docks are loaded with the stone so violently plundered from the hills.

To an observer cursed with an over active imagination, looking northwards from Breidden Hill it must have seemed as if all the fires of hell were being vented here.

Today nature, as always, is reclaiming its own. Swans nest in the former dock areas of the canal where the water is sweet and clear. A heritage centre, unsigned but unmistakably announced by the tall chimney, commemorates the past. A now silent place save for the bird song, it can be reached by the path close to the British Waterways depot. Here at least as I write, you must take the informal perambulation. No formal regimented display, no graphically presented information boards, no guide book, just a walk round an industrial archaeological site dominated by the tall brick chimney, a tribute in itself to the bricklayers and steeplejacks skills ...and courage, it is a square structure, metal banded rising a 100 feet or more to its gradually tapering top. The remains of old buildings subdued under the stranglehold of the relentless ivy are scarcely visible except for the fenced off kiln. A huge affair, perhaps 60 feet wide and 120 feet long, an enormous brick beehive whose great fires reduced the stone to agricultural lime.

The weathered faces of the great quarry dominate the village

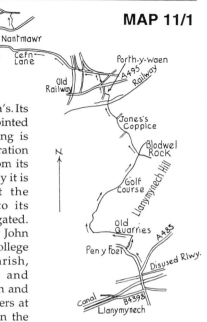

MAP 11/1

and those familiar with the west country might be moved to compare it with the cliffs of the Cheddar Gorge.

Back in the village is the church on the dyke, St Agatha's. Its first rector was Madoc, appointed in 1254, but today's building is mainly the product of a restoration of 1844 and best viewed from its upper gallery. Unaccountably it is to this upper floor that the memorials dating prior to its rebuilding have been relegated. They include one to the Rev John Winn Clark, fellow of Jesus College Oxford, rector of the parish, prependary of St Asaph and Chichester, rector of Corwen and one of His Majesty's preachers at Whitehall who died 1745. In the churchyard are several tombs of the Asterley family, one remembering two daughters, Sarah and Hannah, and another in cast iron with an angel flourishing a trumpet.

LLANYMYNECH TO NANTMAWR

From the canal bridge follow North Road, the A483, as far as the Shropshire boundary sign. Here bear left on the climbing lane signed Pen y Foel which soon opens out to a view of the complex of long quarry faces of Llanymynech Hill which dwarf the brick and white painted houses on the lower slopes.

Continue with the lane as it curves right past the Coach House, where one year blue tits had nested in the mail box on the roadside fence. Pen y Foel cottage displays a "Campers Welcome" notice. Beyond the cottage bear right climbing past houses to meet and cross a stile by a Steetly PLC "Keep to the paths" notice. (The route of the ODP round the quarry area is well waymarked.) Beyond a further stile follow the narrow path through

151

trees which opens out to a view of the quarry and in 80 yards turn left on a rising path. It may well have been one of the inclines that carried stone away from the quarry face.

A sharp climb brings you to a waymark post and a crossing path; turn left over a stile to take the path which terraces the hillside and keep the quarried area to your right throughout. About 20 yards beyond the stile bear left and in 80 yards diagonally right on the narrow path which climbs gently under the long cliffs. In late April and May keep an eye open for the orchids which flourish here in some numbers in this limestone soil.

The path continues through an overgrown area, a touch of the wilderness as nature recovers the ground temporarily lost to it. Man has left successive imprints on Llanymynech Hill, a hill fort the largest in Wales and reputed to be yet another where Caractacus fought his last battle with the Romans. Offa built his dyke along the western edges, quarrying has taken place for perhaps as much as 2,000 years and now the hill accommodates a golf course.

The ODP follows the western side of the golf course, briefly along one edge before plunging under the trees, birch and pine, with Offa's Dyke providing an extra unofficial bunker with the occasional trodden-in ball to be seen. The path returns to edge the fairway, climbing a bank and on to pass a clump of larch trees as the course is left behind. Continue with the path under the trees with the hill falling sharply away on the left until it dips down to meet a crossing path. The dyke continues over Blodwel Rocks, but the ODP leaves it at this point.

Turn sharp left over a stile and descend through the woodland on a winding path with views to the green hills broken by the scarred faces of Blodwel and Llynclys Quarries.

On reaching a stile head diagonally right over the field towards Jones's Coppice. Beyond a further stile turn sharp left joining a rutted track to meet and pass through a gateway to a farm lane. Turn right with the track which passes through the woodland. As the track swings sharp right, leave it and go forward to a metal gateway and stile. (A sign here advertises bed and breakfast at the Red Lion 400 yards to the right.)

Cross the stile and descend the field with the hedge to your left. At the bottom of the field bear slightly diagonally right to a stile and over an old railway line, and then half right over a field to cross a brook.

Go forward with the hedge to your left and bear left with it to meet a stile and turn right into a lane to meet the road (A495) at Porth-y-Waen. Cross the road to the track opposite and in a few yards turn left over a stile and bear half right over a field to the angle of a wire fence. Bear right with the fence to a stile and follow a fenced and hedged path between houses to meet a road and turn left.

At a Y-junction take the forward (ie. left) fork and continue over a crossroads, signed Bryn and Cefn Blodwel. After crossing a stream and disused railway line keep with the rising Cefn Lane for well over ½ mile. When the gateway to Cefn Farm, with its long stone barn, is reached turn right over a stile and descend the field with the hedge to your right. Beyond a stile, found a little way in from the bottom corner of the field, descend through a short patch of woodland to meet a lane and turn right towards the scatter of houses that form Nantmawr village.

MAP 11/2

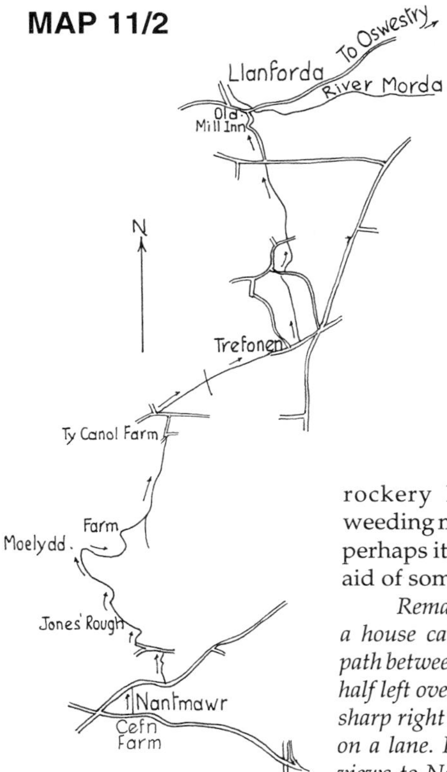

NANTMAWR TO THE OLD MILL INN AND MORDA BRIDGE LLANFORDA

The houses of Nantmawr are set on the hillside and provide problems for some of its gardeners. A solution has been found at the former School House where a fine rockery has been constructed; weeding must still be a problem and perhaps it is accomplished with the aid of some gentle abseiling.

Remain with the road and opposite a house called Kalushi take a hedged path between houses. Beyond a stile bear half left over the field to a stile and then sharp right up the hillside and turn left on a lane. Here there are retrospective views to Nantmawr and Llanymynech

Hill.

When the lane divides in a short distance take the right fork. Shortly after passing the virginia creeper covered Mount Zion the lane becomes a rougher track climbing between trees. Shortly turn right over a stile into Jones' Rough, a nature reserve managed by the Shropshire Wild Life Trust and the Shropshire Trust for Nature Conservation. An information board gives details of birds and flowers to be seen according to season.

A narrow path climbs through the woodland to meet a stile. Go forward over rough but more open ground. In a short distance bear right at a Y-junction of grassy paths to meet a waymarked stile. From here go forward with enclosed fields to your left following a rough track. Beyond a white farmhouse continue on the grassy track shortly leaving the fence line to climb between bracken. Just short of the top of the bank bear right up the hillside climbing on a well waymarked track which curves left to the grassy summit of Moelydd marked by a concrete structure and a large iron pole. Some carefully thought out signing of the ODP directs the northbound walker along the grassy plateau with the path soon falling gently through grass, gorse and bracken to a clear white track.

Bear left and in about 100 yards turn left over a stile and continue with the track towards the farmhouse of Moelydd Uchaf. As the farm gate is reached bear right to follow the field edge to reach a stile and gateway. Bear half left on the track passing through light woodland.

Continue with the track to a gateway passing Ty Canol Farm on your left and on by a narrow lane to meet and turn left on a road. In 30 paces cross a stile on the right and bear half right over the field along a broken line of trees to descend to a stile. Walk ahead with the fence line to your right to cross a stream and stile.

Go ahead with hedge to your left rising gently to a gateway and forward on a metalled lane, passing some attractive houses on the southern edge of Trefonen. In about 300 yards bear left on the lane by a house called Offa's View. Cross a further lane to follow a hedged path to continue on a metalled track past houses to cross a stile into a lane.

Continue through a small enclosure by a farm and over a stile to head up the hillside to the top corner of the field to converge with Offa's Dyke. Turn left into a lane, then almost immediately right to follow the field boundary on your right to reach a strip of woodland. Cross a stile and go forward on the dyke now with the fenceline to your left. A good section of the dyke diminishes in height as the road is reached near Pentre-shannel.

Turn left and shortly right descending steeply to the valley of the Morda by the former Llanforda Mill, now The Old Mill Inn.

THE OLD MILL INN LLANFORDA TO OSWESTRY

At the road junction turn right crossing the bridge over the River Morda, the ODP is signed off left by a white house. For Oswestry follow the narrow rising lane for just over a mile. At a T-junction turn left, signed Old Racecourse. In 300 yards turn right, Broomhall Lane but not named at this point, and keep with it for over 1/2 mile passing the waterworks and at the next junction turn left via Upper Brook Lane to reach the town centre.

*The spirit of border farming
depicted in this fine bronze at Oswestry*

12: The Last of The Dyke
Oswestry to Llangollen

MAPS:	1:25,000 Pathfinder	847 (SJ 22/32)
		827 (SJ 23/33)
		806 (SJ 24/34)
	1:50,000 Landranger	126 Shrewsbury
		117 Chester & Wrexham

FACILITIES: Shops, refreshments and accommodation at Oswestry, Froncysyllte and Llangollen. Excellent tea rooms at Chirk Castle during summer opening hours.

PARKING FOR ROUND WALKS: Oswestry Old Racecourse; off road, Panorama Walk, Llangollen.

MILEAGE CHARTS:

Oswestry to regain ODP	2¹⁄₂	
The Old Mill, Llanforda to Craignant	4¹⁄₂	4¹⁄₂
Craignant to Castle Mill for Chirk Castle	1³⁄₄	1³⁄₄
Castle Mill to Tyn-y-groes via Chirk Castle, summer only	(4/5)	
Castle Mill to Tyn-y-groes	1	1
Tyn-y-groes to Froncysyllte	3	3
Froncysyllte via Aqueduct to link with original ODP	³⁄₄	
Froncysyllte via bridge		³⁄₄
To Llangollen via the canal	4	
Official route via Panorama Walk		4
Totals	17¹⁄₂	15

The alternatives on offer are less complicated on the ground than they appear on the page and are fully detailed in the main text.

It is in this section that the walker must bid farewell to Offa's Dyke as the ODP leaves it near the Llangollen Canal to take a more westerly line than the old Mercian frontier. After rejoining the route of the ODP from Oswestry the dyke is followed through the woodland of Craig Forda. The ODP leaves the earthwork to cross the old racecourse but rejoins it at Carreg-y-big then deserts it again as the path follows the western edge of Selattyn Hill. Beyond Craignant there are good sections of the dyke particularly on the descent to Bronygarth. After the crossing of the Ceiriog the dyke takes a line, albeit broken, through the grounds of Chirk Castle but the ODP does not link with it save for a brief, almost unnoticed, section as it makes for the Dee valley near Pentre. The course of the dyke thereafter to Prestatyn is today intermittent and forms no part of the ODP.

Whilst by no means level the walking is not hard going but in planning their itinerary walkers should give consideration to the inclusion of a visit to Chirk Castle (for opening times see the Useful Information section). The alternative routes to Llangollen from Froncysyllte are given for completeness but the crossing of the Dee by Telford's remarkable aqueduct is recommended in preference to the original route. At the end of a long day the towpath to Llangollen is both easy going and enjoyable. Nevertheless the views from the Panorama Walk and Castell Dinas Bran are superb, if ending your journey at Llangollen then this is the route to take. Those continuing northwards after an overnight stop in the town will find the hill top fort and a section of the Panorama Walk are included in the following day's schedule, so nothing is lost by taking the canalside route.

OSWESTRY

All the border towns visited so far, with the exception of Kington, have been in Wales, even Kington lies on the western side of Offa's frontier. That Oswestry is in England is not in doubt but once it could have been No Mans Land for Offa's Dyke is well to the west of the town and Wat's Dyke ran through the hill fort on its eastern edge leaving the castle site and the centre of today's town between the two.

The Old Oswestry hill fort occupies the site of a village dating back nearly 3,000 years around which its late iron age residents constructed over the course of several centuries a complicated series of ramparts - seven in all. Some still water filled pits on the western side of the fort seemed to have been dug to solve the problem common to later inhabitants of stone castles who were as likely to be defeated by thirst as much as a direct onslaught. Today it looks out over the cricket pitches to the town and provides an interesting circuit aided by a number of information points.

Some of Oswestry's history has already been touched upon in the introductory chapter describing the growth of the Mercian kingdom. It was here in AD642 that Penda defeated the Northumbrian army led by their Christian king Oswald. Herein lies the origin of the town's name. Following the battle Penda is said to have impaled Oswald's head on a stake, another account says he was crucified on a tree. Giraldus, always eager to record past events, briefly refers in his *Journey Through Wales,* to an overnight stop at Oswestry which he explains was named the Tree of the Saint Oswald. The saint is also connected with one of the frequent legends that are attached to wells. In this instance an eagle is supposed to have snatched up one of the king's severed limbs. The grisly prize proved too heavy for the bird and it fell to the ground where a spring at once gushed forth. The site is marked on the map on the south-western edge of the town, coincidentally not so very far from the modern waterworks.

A town trail leaflet available from the Tourist Information Office provides an interesting insight into the history of many of Oswestry's old buildings. A lofty view of the town may be enjoyed from the castle site, found behind the Guildhall. Little of the castle, dating from pre-Norman times, remains today just a scatter of stones at the top of an earthern mound reached by a winding path. The town's adherence to the royalist cause ensured its destruction after the Civil War. Once a walled town the pillars of one of the gateways are set at the foot of the mound and the words Toll Free can just about be made out.

One of Oswestry's best preserved buildings, at the corner of Cross Street and Bailey Street, is the handsome timber framed Llwyd Mansion of 1604, the home of a wealthy merchant. Wool was of course an important part of the town's trade and in Smithfield the spirit of this border country is encapsulated in a fine bronze by Ivor Roberts Jones. It depicts in graphic detail a stockily built farmer with what must surely be his prize horned ram. Nothing could be more appropriate for throughout the long history of the region one thing has remained constant for perhaps 4,000 years - sheep farming.

The Old Grammar School, founded in 1407 by David Holbache,

is now an heritage centre. Its exhibits include a section on the Crimean War seen through the eyes of local men and women, the usual selection of farming implements expected in rural communities and a reconstructed school room. A slice of advertising history is represented in the collection of the enamelled signs which between the years 1880 and 1950 were used to promote such household products as Sussex rubber soles and heels, Liptons tea, BSA bicycles, Wild Woodbine cigarettes and the ubiquitous Virol.

Close by is the parish church of St Oswalds, of almost cathedral like proportions and badly damaged during the Civil War. Amongst its memorials is one to Hugh Yale a relative of the founder of Yale University in the USA. In Broad Walk by the church is a plaque installed in March 1993 to commemorate the centenary of an Oswestry man, the war poet Wilfred Owen. He won a Military Cross in October 1918 and within seven days of the Armistice was killed whilst supervising his men bridging a canal. Quotations from two of his poems, Futility and Anthem for Doomed Youth convey the depth of his experience. In the last he asks "What passing-bells for those who die as cattle? and answers " - Only the monstrous anger of the guns, Only the stuttering rifles' rapid rattle, Can patter out their hasty orisons...".

Another of the town's famous sons was Sir Henry Walford Davies, whose distinguished musical career was crowned with his appointment as Master of the King's Music in 1934.

Oswestry enjoyed a period as one of Britain's famous railway towns, as the headquarters of Cambrian Railways. At one time the engineering works employed some 2,000 men in the construction and maintenance of engines and rolling stock. Some 73 steam locomotives operated from the Oswestry sheds. A dual museum in Station Yard reflects the story of both steam and pedal power. The history of the Cambrian Railways is presented with exhibits large and small. A programme of events recalls the celebrations to mark the start of the work on the Oswestry, Ellesmere and Whitchurch section of the railway in 1862. The whole town seems to have been involved with a great procession of bands and local organisations trooping out to watch the cutting of the first sod. Amongst the engines a warning notice on the wall cautions visitors to "Beware of Rail Enthusiast's Disease, highly infectious to males of all ages...".

The Bicycle Museum which shares the same premises has a collection of over a hundred different models ranging from a bone shaker of 1868 to the cycles of the 1940s. Rarest item in the collection is a solid tyred Quadrant dwarf safety bicycle, made in 1889, only four are known to exist in the British Isles.

From Oswestry the ODP heads north to leave Shropshire and into Glyndwr Country from which the District Council covering the towns of Llangollen, Ruthin, Denbigh, Corwen and Chirk takes its name.

OWAIN GLYNDWR

To many Owain Glyndwr must seem a shadowy mysterious figure, almost mythical, a man in the mould of an Arthur or a Robin Hood and thus one of the great folk heroes of history. He may be perceived as a leader of a guerilla band raiding the English border, a robber baron, a poor man seeking justice or a revolutionary leader rallying his people to the flag of freedom. Some of these perceptions are ill conceived, some contain an element of truth. Mythical he is not, much of his story is well recorded even if the facts are subject to differing interpretations. Such mystery that surrounds him is not so much in his presence front stage in the history of the late fourteenth and early fifteenth centuries but in his life and death thereafter. Certainly he was not a poor man seeking justice but rather a rich man in pursuit of the same Holy Grail, and as events and maybe his ambition dictated, a man set to assume the mantle of the Prince of Wales.

Glyndwr was born a Welshman of the borders circa 1359, at Sycarth a few miles south-west of Oswestry, a son of a wealthy family descended from the Princes of Powys. He studied law in London and in 1385 joined Richard II's unsuccessful expedition against the Scots. No sign of the rebel here, the resort to arms was yet but the smallest of black clouds upon a distant horizon despite the perennial atmosphere of dissatisfaction that prevailed throughout Wales.

The match that was to light the fuse to the eventual great explosion can be found in the disputed ownership of land held by the neighbouring Lord Grey of Ruthin. In 1400 or thereabouts, Glyndwr took his case to an arrogant, unsympathetic Parliament

The River Morda,
near Llanforda Mill

Right:
The River Dee, Llangollen

Looking north to Moel Fammau, from Moel Fenlli
A view to the sea from the Meliden Quarries, near Prestatyn

and returned home a discontented man with the bitter words "What care we for these barefoot dogs" ringing in his ears. He was hardly a man to whom these deadly words could be applied or in any way merited whatever the rights of his claim and they must have lingered long as hurt to be avenged: words that were to cost the marcher lords dear in lost revenues and Glyndwr even more in the capture of one son, the death of another and the loss of his lands.

The smouldering fuse was fanned to a fiercer flame by yet another problem with Grey who accused him of being a traitor for his failure to support Henry IV's war with Scotland. A serious charge, the fault was not Glyndwr's but that of Grey who had, deliberately or otherwise, been late in summoning Owain's support.

The fuse fizzed to its first small explosion as Glyndwr launched a murderous raid upon Grey's properties, from which a greater powder trail led to an entire arsenal of gunpowder that was to set Wales and the border country ablaze for a decade of death and destruction. Towns were plundered and burnt, crops destroyed and cattle stolen as successive English armies failed to bring to account an exceptionally skilled and elusive foe.

The revolt spread through a discontented nation, Glyndwr's fellow Welsh landowners joined him, students at the English seats of learning returned home to join the fight, humble labourers willingly joined the cause; even the clergy and the monastic foundations pledged their support - at some cost as it turned out. Castles and towns fell before Owain's angry men. When Henry sent an army against him, Owain simply laid low until his enemy was defeated by their own depleted supplies. Some sort of uneasy peace descended as Glyndwr remained under cover until early in 1401 he was in action again both in the south and north of the country, with considerable if not complete success. Attempts at a peaceful outcome, whether genuine or not, came to naught and Glyndwr looked for allies in the Irish, the Scots and the French.

Early in 1402 Glyndwr was again raiding Ruthin and later took Grey prisoner; the young and future King Henry V was engaged in repelling raids on Herefordshire and Monmouthshire. The defeat of the English and the "capture?" of Mortimer at Pilleth has already been described. A three pronged attack launched against the Principality in the autumn by a huge army was a disaster, beaten as much by the weather and the terrain as by the Welsh.

By 1403 all but a few of the castles loyal to the crown had succumbed and the rest were under heavy pressure. The young Prince Henry sought to bring Glyndwr to battle but he continued his successful "Will o' the wisp" activity to avoid a head-on confrontation. In the course of that year castles and towns still fell to Glyndwr. The King's troubles were further exacerbated by the revolt of the Percys, defeated at Shrewsbury in July, when the famous son of Northumberland Harry Hotspur was slain. Glyndwr took no part in the battle but was again active in raids along the border counties.

Early in 1404 he launched a sustained but unsuccessful attack on Carnarvon Castle but soon took Harlech and increased his hold on Wales so that it seemed he would indeed assume power over all the land southward from the Mersey to the Severn estuary as promised in an agreement to divide the territory of England and Wales between himself, the Percys and Mortimer.

Successes continued in 1405 but not all the stars shone brightly for Glyndwr, his son was captured and held prisoner in the Tower of London. Assistance from the French had minimal effect and in the following year the tide began to turn against Glyndwr. Little by little resistance faded although Glyndwr using all his old skills remained at large. In 1411 Henry IV pardoned all the rebellious Welshmen save their leader - too bitter a pill to swallow. Fire in the belly does not feed a man's family, farmers must return to tend their land, students to seek honours in other halls of fame. Even the most steadfast of heroes grow weary and look for the gentler warmth of their own hearths rather than the fiercer flames of war. Henry V succeeded to the throne and issued further pardons which this time embraced even Glyndwr. But Glyndwr was never a man to surrender and it was only he that did not finally give way to the offer of pardons and a quieter life. Nevertheless the years of strife had taken their toll and he faded from the scene. At the height of his success there is no question that Glyndwr held Wales in his hands, militarily, politically and above all the hearts of the people. It is strange therefore but wholly in keeping with the years of conflict that where he went and the manner of his death is unclear - an old soldier who faded away. Kilvert in his diary writing of a visit to Monnington-on-

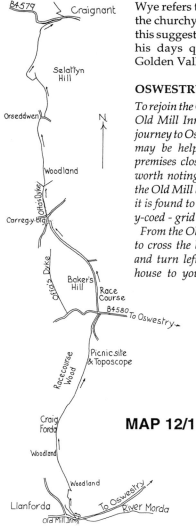

Wye refers to the old warrior buried in the churchyard, but historians dispute this suggesting that he probably ended his days quietly in Herefordshire's Golden Valley.

OSWESTRY TO CRAIGNANT

To rejoin the ODP retrace your steps to The Old Mill Inn as described on the inward journey to Oswestry or as a timesaver a taxi may be helpful - a firm operates from premises close to the main car park. It is worth noting that maps do not designate the Old Mill by name and for identification it is found to the west of the woods at Tyn-y-coed - grid ref: 256282.

From the Old Mill, Llanforda, go forward to cross the bridge over the River Morda and turn left on a track passing a white house to your right. Beyond a gateway continue with the track and soon after passing stone buildings bear half right climbing into broadleaf woodland, mainly beech and oak.

On meeting a crossing path go over, rising more steeply to meet a wide track and turn right. In 30 paces bear left still climbing with the wood falling sharply away to your left and soon with the dyke found as the path levels out to terrace the hillside.

When a path comes in from the right go forward with it

MAP 12/1

The path climbs to the woods of Craig Forda

not far from the top edge of the wood marked on the map as Craig Forda. After a period of level walking bear right to pass through a broken wall then immediately left. The path rises but holds to its northward direction on the inside edge of the wood.

After a short passage with open fields to your right go forward over a stile and continue to reach, in 300 yards, the open ground of the Old Racecourse with its picnic site. (The dyke has already taken a lower course through Racecourse Wood.)

The ODP crosses the Old Racecourse soon meeting a toposcope, installed by the Oswestry Rotary Club, which identifies the hills and mountains in the south and west from this 1,080 feet viewpoint.

It takes a clear day to pick out all those listed but in the southern arc they include Brown Clee 36 miles, Titterstone Clee 35, Caer Caradoc 25 (another supposed site of Caractacus's last battle), The Long Mynd 24, Stiperstones 25, Breidden Hill 13, Moel y Golfa 15, Corndon Hill 22, The Long Mountain 16, Kerry Hill 30 and Pontesbury Hill 24 miles.

The western arc is no less impressive including Plynlimon 35 miles, Cader Idris 35 and Moel Sych - highest point of the Berwyn Mountains at 2,712 feet - 12 miles.

Maintain your northward direction beyond the viewpoint soon with a road running parallel to your right. At the road junction (signed Oswestry to the right) go ahead on the Selattyn road for ³/₄ mile.

The dyke will be seen running over Baker's Hill ¹/₄ mile or so to the west. The road falls to meet a T-junction at Carreg-y-big, where turn right signed Selattyn 1 ¹/₂ miles. In 150 yards turn left up a bank and go forward along the line of the dyke to meet a conifer plantation in 600 yards. Thence over a stile to follow the dyke top along the edge of the woodland.

Beyond the trees follow the field edges at first with a further plantation to your left and the forested top of Selattyn Hill seen ahead. The ODP dips sharply to cross a small stream then over a short field to meet a stile with the buildings of Orseddwen seen to your left.

Go ahead over an open grassy area to meet and turn right on a track soon to cross a cattle grid. Offa's Dyke again takes a divergent course, perhaps deliberately missing the somewhat marshy area which the ODP shortly follows.

About 30 paces beyond the cattle grid turn left on a good track and keep with this as it steadily climbs the hillside to the woodland on the western flanks of Selattyn Hill.

The gated track is good under foot but the ground either side is rough wettish moorland with old stone walls dividing part of the hillside into small fields. Lapwings nest here, on the ground, and a pair were seen driving off a predatory magpie - a persistent plunderer of both eggs and chicks.

Double gates bar the way into the woodland, here cross the stile to the left and bear right along three sides of the field to meet the gateway to an old walled track. Descend with this for ½ mile, merging with the farm lane from Woodside, to meet the B4579 near Craignant.

CRAIGNANT TO CASTLE MILL

On meeting the road turn right and in a few yards fishhook left to descend on a narrow lane to the valley. Bear right after crossing a stream with the remains of an old kiln facing you. Continue, now rising, with the lane to pass Yew Tree House where the metalled lane comes to an abrupt end.

Go forward on a grassy path rising to meet a further lane. Turn left and in a few yards right, over a stile and head up the field passing through a soggy patch and over a streamlet. Shortly turn left climbing slightly to a stile and then turn right on Offa's Dyke. Keep with the dyke to meet another lane where turn right and in a few paces left over a stile to continue north-easterly on the line of the dyke, initially with a plantation to your left.

In just over ¼ mile go over a crossing path and continue with the hedge to your left. At the next stile, in 200 yards, descend on a stepped path through a jungle-like dingle to cross a stream and up the opposite bank. Thence ahead over the field to meet a lane.

Turn right and in a few paces left up a bank to go forward on the top of the dyke. Shortly, after passing a small pool, turn right over a stile and left to follow a narrow tread between the dyke and a wire fence.

Views open out to the various crossings of the valley, including the railway viaduct and the aqueduct which carries the Llangollen branch of the Shropshire Union Canal 70 feet over the river; one of the engineering triumphs of the golden days of inland waterways. Chirk is seen forward right and the billowing smoke from a factory chimney.

The threat to bare legs from the lush vegetation along the dyke is eventually removed as the ODP rises to follow the dyke top.

This is the last good section of the dyke available to the northbound traveller and offers fine views over the Ceiriog Valley and its well wooded hills. The dyke itself has some fine mature beeches and later conifers along its course.

A stretch of level walking leads to a steep descent and over a crossing path. Beyond the stiles go ahead now with the dyke to your left. Several more stiles are crossed where the field is divided by a series of electric fences.

Shortly after passing Gibraltar Cottage the hedgeline falls back but the ODP maintains its direction to meet a gateway and stile. Cross the farm lane (it can be very soggy here) and continue on a hedged path. At the foot of the field turn left on the path and on to meet and cross a road and on over the River Ceiriog to meet the B4500.

From Orseddwed the dyke

MAP 12/2

has marked the modern boundary between England and Wales as far as the river.

The options on this section of the walk now come into play.

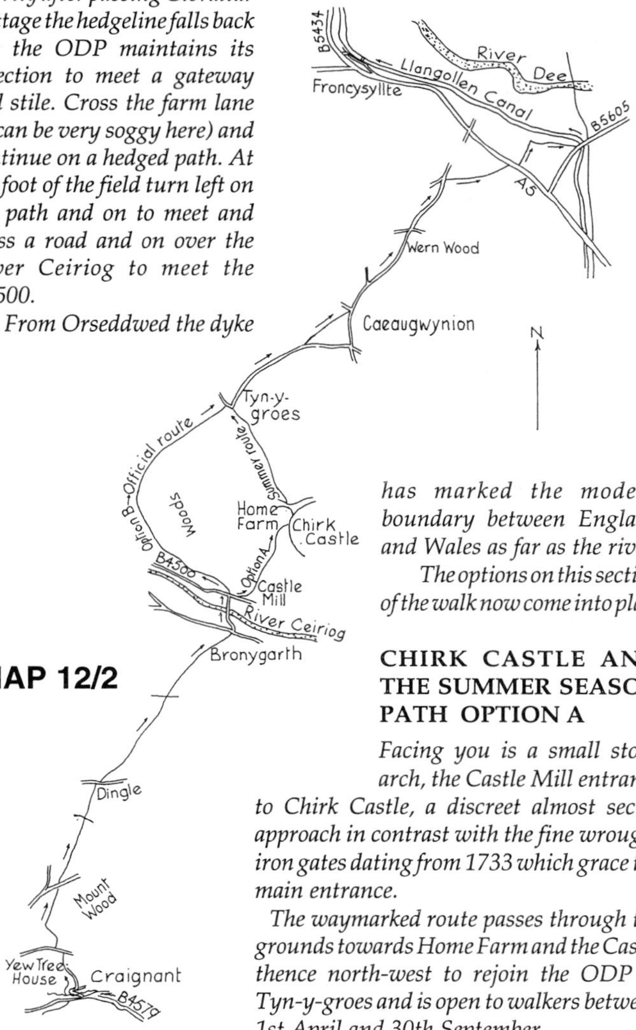

CHIRK CASTLE AND THE SUMMER SEASON PATH OPTION A

Facing you is a small stone arch, the Castle Mill entrance to Chirk Castle, a discreet almost secret approach in contrast with the fine wrought iron gates dating from 1733 which grace the main entrance.

The waymarked route passes through the grounds towards Home Farm and the Castle thence north-west to rejoin the ODP at Tyn-y-groes and is open to walkers between 1st April and 30th September.

Chirk Castle from the gardens

CHIRK CASTLE

The castle is set in extensive parkland where cattle and sheep graze beneath mature trees. Without, the castle still demonstrates all the strengths of the medieval stronghold, within, all the grandeur of a stately home. Thus its two roles are combined in a history that has treated it less harshly than many another castle.

Round towers project from the massive stone walls, improving visibility and fire power; within the secure central courtyard a 100-foot deep well ensured the garrison would not lack water however long it might be under siege. The castle was built close to the end of the thirteenth century, one of the chain constructed in the reign of Edward I designed to impose his sovereignty upon Wales. It was purchased by Sir Thomas Myddleton in 1595, remaining in the family's hands for nearly 400 years.

Sir Thomas prospered from his trading activities with the East India Company. In 1630 he was associated with an early publication of a Welsh language bible. His younger brother, Hugh, also had an interesting history. Born in 1560, he went to London to take up a career as a goldsmith and banker and was in partnership with Sir Walter Raleigh in overseas ventures. As a clothier he gave employment to several hundred workers but is best known for his enterprise in bringing a supply of fresh water to the capital. It was an ambitious and costly project. The work began in 1609 with the New River 10 feet deep and 4 feet wide engineered to carry water from springs in the Hertfordshire villages of Amwell and Chadwell to a reservoir at Clerkenwell a distance of nearly 40 miles. From Clerkenwell the water was fed to the city in wooden conduits with lead pipes feeding individual houses.

The scheme encountered much opposition and just about drained Myddleton of his resources; further financing was ultimately provided by James I in return for a share of the profits. The work was completed in 1613 with the official opening ceremony performed by Hugh's brother, Thomas, the Lord Mayor of London. It proved to be a profitable venture and was to continue, with improvements, to supply water to the capital into the twentieth century.

A tour of the castle begins in the Cromwell Room where a large collection of Civil War weapons is displayed. This serves to introduce the visitor to another Sir Thomas Myddleton (1586-1666). He was MP for the county (Denbigh) during the Civil War and a strong supporter of the Parliamentary cause. When hostilities broke out the castle was seized by the Royalists whilst its owner was away from home. Myddleton seems to have exercised considerable military skills during the campaigns that were fought in the north of Wales where he held a command as Major General. He raised the Royalists siege of Oswestry in 1644 and in September of that year captured Newtown and effected the apparently bloodless surrender of Montgomery Castle. The Royalist commander at Shrewsbury launched a counter-offensive and laid siege to the castle while Myddleton was assembling a larger army. In mid-September a battle close to Montgomery decisively defeated the Royalists. Within two weeks Myddleton had captured Powis Castle and moved on to besiege the Royalists in Shrewsbury. Ironically, despite these successes, he was unable to relieve his own castle at Chirk.

After his death in 1658 Cromwell's son Richard succeeded him as the Lord Protector. In the following year Myddleton joined the uprising led by Sir George Booth to rally support for the restoration of the monarchy. The successful capture of the City of Chester in August was quickly reversed in a defeat at Nantwich by the Parliamentarian general, John Lambert. Booth was captured and imprisoned in the Tower of London. Lambert went on to attack Chirk Castle which Myddleton was obliged to surrender.

Sir Thomas Myddleton was then 73 years old, but lived to receive the tangible gratitude of Charles II with the gift of a fine cabinet reputed to have cost for those days the enormous sum of £10,000.

A tour of the house will also reward the visitor with its fine furniture and furnishings. One item that will certainly catch the eye is the exceptionally large long case clock, 10 feet 8 inches high, the work of a local clock maker.

OPTION B
CEIRIOG BRIDGE, CHIRK TO TYN-Y-GROES

While a visit to the National Trust's Chirk Castle is recommended, out of the summer opening season the official route of the ODP must be taken; this swings in a semi-circle round the western side of the estate with a distant view to the castle.

Having crossed the bridge over the River Ceiriog to reach the B4500, take the single track "No Through Road" opposite the junction. The lane climbs the hillside between wooded banks thick with ramsons (wild garlic) in early summer and regaining some of the height lost on your descent to the Ceiriog Valley. As a track comes in from the right continue forward and at a Y-junction bear right, climbing past the white houses at Ty Brickly. Continue beyond a gateway and passing farm buildings head up the hillside with a stone wall to your left and woodland to your right.

After the path levels out leave the woodland by turning right over a stile found by a large oak tree to go ahead to a marker post at the angle of a stone wall. Continue up the hillside soon joining a trackway to reach a stile and gateway. Go forward over pasture with Chirk Castle seen on the hill to your right and descend gently towards the stile and house seen ahead.

Beyond the stile follow a clear track passing the house to meet a road at a sharp angle and turn right. At this point the alternative path through Chirk Park rejoins the official route.

TYN-Y-GROES TO FRONCYSYLLTE

Keep with the road for nearly ¹/₂ mile, passing The Kennels. About 100 yards beyond a poplar plantation turn left over a stile to cross a field diagonally right to a stile and over a narrow fenced area. Maintain the slight diagonal course gently up the hillside to a stile and metal gate and turn right to meet the lane opposite the farm buildings of Caeaugwynion.

Turn left with the lane and at a Y-junction take the right fork descending to pass Fron Cottage. This is yet another lane rich in bankside wild flowers. Continue over minor crossroads and in ¹/₄ mile leave the lane by a stile found on the right. Head slightly right over the field and through gap in the hedge to descend half left over the field passing under power lines to meet a stile at the far corner.

Follow the field boundary (on your right) to cross a stile set in a stone wall to meet the A5 and turn right. In 30 yards or so turn left on a wide track, climbing gently to meet a metal gate and stile. Continue with fenceline to your right with the houses and factories of Trevor and Cefn-Mawr coming into view on the hillside. This is the very last section of the dyke the walker will follow.

At the end of the field cross a stile, and bear half right through the hedgerow to cross the field to a further broken boundary. Maintain your direction over the field on a narrow tread to meet the road B5605 and turn left over the canal bridge at Pentre.

Turn left to follow the towpath of the Llangollen Canal for a mile to the white painted swing bridge at Froncysyllte. The canal is set well above the Dee and the long viaduct carrying the railway over the valley will be seen through breaks in the trees that line the bank.

As Froncysyllte is reached alternative routes are on offer.

OPTION C

This is the original route of the ODP which gives impressive views to the aqueduct but without the pleasure of the high crossing of the Dee. It is described for the sake of completeness but Option D is recommended.

Cross the swing bridge and turn right along the canal with the Aqueduct Inn seen above you. Leave the canal after a short distance to bear left and then sharp right onto the road (B5434), which descends to cross the Dee by the narrow bridge.

Keep with the road climbing to meet houses where turn left up a stepped path to reach the canal and turn left with the towpath to meet a footbridge in 40 yards. The continuation of the official route is described in Option F.

OPTION D

On meeting the swing bridge at Fronsycyllte continue with the towpath which soon curves to cross the River Dee by the famous aqueduct, a mild adventure for the walker or canal enthusiast and another triumph of the waterways age.

The work is that of Thomas Telford, arguably the greatest engineer of his day (1757-1834). The son of a Scottish shepherd, on leaving school learnt the stonemason's skills and after a period in Edinburgh, London and Portsmouth, was appointed Surveyor of Public Works for Shropshire. He was engaged on work with the Ellesmere Canal for twelve years from 1793. The construction of the aqueduct, completed in 1805, required the building of some 18 piers to support the 1,007 feet long iron trough which took the canal 126 feet at its highest point over the Dee. The not unexciting crossing provided a slim towpath and a channel 5 feet 3 inches deep with a bare inch or two of freeway for the narrow boats. The troughs were made at the local Cefn-Mawr and Shrewsbury foundries of the ironmaster William Hazeldine.

The view over the Dee valley from the towpath is superb and the modern road crossing already glimpsed on the way from Pentre would have surely delighted Telford with its almost delicate use of concrete.

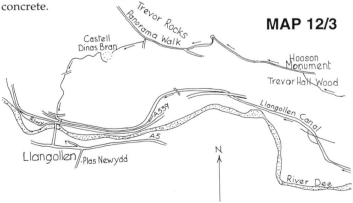

MAP 12/3

On reaching the northern end of the aqueduct descend by the path found immediately on the right to pass under the last span of the aqueduct and climb again to meet the road and turn right. Cross the canal bridge and turn left along the towpath. In 100 yards cross a footbridge and continue with the towpwath to meet a further bridge, having rejoined the route described in Option C.

(Note - a little beyond the aqueduct is the canal basin with an information board on the restoration of the canal, shop and boat trips).

There are now two possible routes to Llangollen.

OPTION E

After a long day, with time spent at Chirk Castle, the quickest way to Llangollen may well be preferred. If this is so, simply keep with the pleasant towpath for the 4 miles to Llangollen. The canal continues on a carefully engineered course high above the Vale of Llangollen with views to

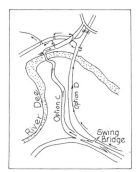

a green landscape of woods and fields dotted by farms and the occasional white painted house. The Dee is often as not invisible while to the right there are views to the mountainous terrain with Castell Dinas Bran seen ahead ruined but still in command of the Vale. The canal is cut close to the rock face, in places leaving space only for the passage of a single narrow boat. In summer curlews call from the meadows below. As you approach the town a long line of narrow boats may be moored for the Llangollen arm of the Shropshire Union Canal is very popular with the boating fraternity.

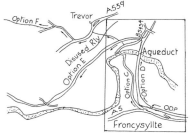

On reaching the bridge by

The canal carried 126 feet above the Dee by Telford's Froncysyllte Aqueduct

the canal centre, descend Wharf Hill and into the town via the ancient bridge which spans the more turbulent waters of the Dee.

OPTION F

This is the official route of the ODP and will take you to Llangollen via the Panorama Walk and Castell Dinas Bran. Since this also forms the route of the outward journey from Llangollen the superb views from this hill top fortress will not be lost if you opt for the towpath. A section of the Panorama Walk is also included in the next day's itinerary.

Cross the footbridge over the canal (ie. this is the second footbridge after leaving the aqueduct route, Option D, or the first if using the swing bridge route, Option C).

From the northern side of the canal make your way half left over a field to meet a stile where turn left to follow the railway embankment shortly to pass through a narrow tunnel under the disused railway. Turn right and in a few yards bear left on a tarmac path to reach a road (A539).

Turn left and in 300 yards turn right on a minor road to reach a house called Gardeners Lodge in 350 yards. Take the broad tree-lined track on the left and in about 80 yards bear right up the hillside on a narrow and sometimes rocky path through mixed woodland. On meeting a stile at the top of the rise go ahead on the outside edge of the wood with a stone wall to your left to meet a stile. Re-enter woodland and go forward on a wide but dark descending tunnel-like path. At a narrow Y-junction ignore the left fork and keep ahead through a more open area, now following power lines with a line of rocks to your left.

At a further junction continue forward on a narrow path making a long steep climb through Trevor Wood - conifer and broadleaf. On meeting the single track road which forms part of the famous Panorama Walk turn left.

A monument on the hillside remembers I.D.Hooson "..1880-1948 Bardd, Eisteddfodwr. Cyfaili. Iblant. Cymru": a bard honoured by his fellow Welshmen and despoiled on one side by mindless graffiti. From this spot there is a fine view to the ruins of Castell Dinas Bran, atmospherically Arthurian in aspect from this distance as its ruined towers reach out to the lowering clouds. A sight that must surely have stirred the imagination of the writers and poets who made the pilgrimage to Wales to visit the "Ladies of Llangollen" - among them Sir Walter Scott - not a man to pass up a good castle.

The Panorama Walk is followed for 1½ miles to the foot of the hill that bears Castell Dinas Bran on its strong shoulders. (Note take care not to be diverted onto the lane that fish-hooks left at a sharp bend but maintain your north-westerly direction.)

The prospect is all that might be expected, high cliff and scree to your right leading on to Trevor Rocks and as the trees fall back the valley of the Dee with Llangollen set beneath the wooded hills.

The ODP continues beyond Castell Dinas Bran but for Llangollen leave the Panorama Walk to turn left on a narrow lane. In a few yards turn right over a stile and take the waymarked route to the summit castle. After enjoying the superb views take the path from the southern side of the ramparts which falls westward on the waymarked winding path. The path swings south descending to the canal and Wharf Hill thence to cross the Dee bridge into the town centre.

13: The Panorama Walk
Llangollen to Pen-y-stryt

MAPS: 1:25,000 Pathfinder   806 (SJ 24/34)
                                789 (SJ 25/35) (small section)
                                788 (SJ 05/15) (minute section)
         1:50,000 Landranger   117 Chester & Wrexham
                                116 Denbigh & Colwyn Bay (extreme
                                eastern edge)

FACILITIES: Shops, refreshments and accommodation at Llangollen, and
    in the Llandegla area.

PARKING FOR ROUND WALKS: Llangollen; off road on the Panorama
    Walk: World's End - car park found at the woodland edge to the north.

MILEAGE CHART:
Llangollen to rejoin route at Trevor Rocks via Castell Dinas Bran   1¼
Trevor Rocks to World's End   3½
World's End to Pen-y-stryt   3¾
_____
Total (ODP route only 7¼)   8½

This section follows the official route throughout apart from the link from
Llangollen.

The varied nature of the ODP is well represented in the northward
route from Llangollen. The walk has sustained scenic interest
offering a splendid viewpoint from an ancient castle set high above
the Vale, a narrow path over scree slopes, the crossing of a lonely
stretch of moorland and a descent through woodland and green
fields.

Walkers who have opted to follow the long distance route in
shorter sections will find Llangollen an excellent base from which
to launch out on the final 35 miles to Prestatyn. It will be no less
attractive to those who have already covered many miles and
would welcome a day's respite. Both will find much to interest them
in and around the town.

LLANGOLLEN

Llangollen is a superb small Welsh market town situated on the banks of the delightful River Dee and under the ancient fort of Castell Dinas Bran. Once reliant on the flannel industry it is now very much orientated to the tourist trade particularly so in July with its now famous International Musical Eisteddfod. The event has gone from strength to strength since its inauguration in 1947. Competitors from all over the world now perform in the Royal Pavilion an acoustically fine concert hall completed in 1993 which can be extended to accommodate an audience of 7,000.

The bridge over the Dee was once known as one of the seven wonders of Wales and the early crossing of this never still river was certainly an achievement. The present bridge dates in part from the fourteenth century but there seems to have been a bridge at this point 200 years earlier. Given the turbulent nature of the river the structure must have been in need of almost constant attention. Today the bridge is a popular place for visitors to view the river as

River Dee and the Llangollen Railway - nostalgic steam hauled trips

The chain bridge over the Dee upstream from Llangollen
Plas Newydd - the home of the Ladies of Llangollen for fifty years

it tumbles in a rush of white water to a deep salmon pool.

On its northern side the Llangollen Railway Society runs nostalgic steam hauled trips following the river to Berwyn. At the nearby Llangollen Wharf the urgent whistle of locomotive and the rhythmic rattle of steel wheels on iron tracks gives way to a quieter but no less nostalgic progress as passengers glide beneath the green canopy of the trees lulled by the soporific lap of water against the sides of horse drawn barges.

The canal has its birth some 3 miles upstream where Thomas Telford constructed a graceful weir, now more romantically known as the Horseshoe Falls, to hold back the onward rush of the Dee to provide a feeder for the man made waterway. Close by is the Chain Bridge near the Berwyn station of the railway. The Dee, always a volatile river, has been partly tamed by flood prevention works near Bala, but not so very old photographs show the bridge being almost overwhelmed by a mountainous rush of water and the streets of Llangollen inundated.

Llangollen owes its name to the founder of its ancient church, St Collen, which should not be missed if only for its splendid hammer beam roof. Here high above your head is a magnificent display of the carpenters and carvers art with numerous carved figures ranging from angels and the madonna and child to musicians, dragons and a woman in a scold's bridle. A recent stained glass window in the porch depicts Collen armed with a gleaming sword - a clean limbed young man engaged in the fight against evil and injustice. Giving up the sword he went to Glastonbury to learn the arts of more peaceful persuasion. After years of monastic study the saint now armoured with "the sword of the spirit" travelled to Wales and in about AD600 founded a small chapel on the site of the present church.

A pictorial memorial in the church shows the widely famed Ladies of Llangollen with high hats, whilst their triangular gravestone is to be found in the churchyard.

"The Ladies" story is an interesting one even when seen in the climate of the twentieth century. We should begin, not in the churchyard of this little Welsh town, but in eighteenth-century Ireland. Lady Eleanor Butler, daughter of the Earl of Ormonde and Ossory, had formed a close attachment to Miss Sarah Ponsonby, a kinswoman of the Earl of Bessborough. In 1774, when Eleanor was aged 30 they left Ireland to set up home together but were "persuaded" to return to their families. A second successful "elopement" brought them to Llangollen where they purchased a substantial cottage Plas Newydd. They were accompanied by their formidable maid servant Mary Caryll.

The two were to live together in complete harmony and devotion for some fifty years and it is said that they never once spent a night away from their home. Their dress has been described as mannish and the menage attracted considerable curiosity so that visitors to the area sought to make their acquaintance. The visitors over the years included such luminaries as the Duke of Wellington, the politicians Edmund Burke and Lord Castlereagh, poets and writers among them Thomas de Quincey, Lord Byron, Wordsworth, Sheridan, Sir Walter Scott and Lady Caroline Lamb. It was not only the British that came to pay their respects, gifts within the house confirm the interest of foreign royalty one of whom was to describe them as the most celebrated virgins in Europe.

Plas Newydd is splendidly situated in fine gardens with the distant Castell Dinas Bran making a final backdrop that varies between that of a benevolent guardian and a menacing giant. The house itself is even more remarkable, adorned within and without with a large quantity of wood carvings and panelling, much of it brought from country houses and churches by the Ladies' visitors. In a word it is unique. The porch is supported by the uprights from what must have been a very large four poster bed and graced by a carved wooden lion brought here by the great Duke of Wellington. The jet black entrance door has carvings of the four evangelists and the Latin inscription "Watch for you know not the hour". The treasures continue within with much oak panelling, marquetry tables in the library, fragments of stained glass set into windows and amongst the figures on the stair a mermaid and another lion. This is their house but what were Eleanor and Sarah really like? Curiosity over their appearance may be satisfied by the portrait secretly painted by Lady Leighton. An excellent taped commentary provides further insights into their history and that of the house in an entertaining presentation.

Whilst memorial tablets can be notoriously misleading, having made the ladies acquaintance at some distance it is perhaps interesting to look again at the inscriptions on the triangular tomb in St Collen's churchyard. Of Lady Eleanor it records "...Endeared to her many friends by an almost unequalled excellence of heart and by manners worthy of her illustrious birth, the admiration and delight of a very numerous acquaintance. From a brilliant vivacity of mind undiminished to the latest period of a prolonged existence. Her amiable condescension and benevolence secured the grateful attachment of those by whom they had been so long and extensively experienced. Her various perceptions crowned by the most pious and cheerful submission to the Divine Will..."

Lady Eleanor died aged 90 in 1829, Sarah, aged 76 was to follow her eighteen months later as her tablet relates "...She did not long survive her beloved companion Lady Eleanor Butler with whom she had lived in this valley for more than half a century of uninterrupted friendship - but they shall no more return to their House...". Their faithful and much regarded servant Mary Carryl had died twenty years earlier and on her monument the ladies praise her virtues in verse expressing their intention to be buried in the same grave: "...Patient, Industrious, Faithful, Generous, Kind, Her conduct left the proudest far behind. Her virtues dignified her humble birth. And raised her mind above this sordid earth. Attachment (Sacred bond of grateful breasts) Extinguished but with life this tomb attests, Reared by Two Friends who will her loss bemoan, Till with Her Ashes Here shall rest Their own."

George Borrow, that chatty travel writer much given to quoting apparently verbatim his many conversations, spent a great deal of time in Llangollen, recording his adventures in *Wild Wales*, a substantial book published in 1862. It is perhaps more interesting to dip into Borrow after rather than before visiting the area, since a retrospective reading of familiar territory adds more life to his words. He makes references to the flannel industry still flourishing at that time and the glow in the night sky from the furnaces of Cefn Mawr, the slate quarries with their product being carried by canal as far as London. Borrow enjoyed his food and wrote with enthusiasm of a leg of Welsh mutton cooked in herbs gathered from the Berwyn Mountains and of the salmon which seems to have been in good supply.

Two miles from Llangollen, on the road that leads to the justly famous views from the Horseshoe Pass lies the Valle Crucis Abbey, not unlike Tintern in appearance and location. Founded in AD1201 by Madog Ap Gruffydd Maelor, Prince of Northern Powys, and the last Cistercian monastery to be established in the principality. It lies beneath the steep brown/green hills close to a little river and prospered greatly from the woollen trade. After the dissolution it suffered the fate of so many other monasteries that were not suitably located to serve the local population as a church. Today it stands a dignified largely roofless ruin, unique in Wales in having the sole remaining monastic fishpond.

Close by and found a few yards off the main road is Eliseg's Pillar, a now truncated cross erected in the mid ninth century by King Cyngen, to honour Eliseg, his great grandfather who recaptured Powys from the English.

A detailed description of the pillar and its now illegible inscription is provided in the guide to Valle Crucis Abbey which took its name from the monument - the Valley of the Cross.

Valle Crucis Abbey near Llangollen

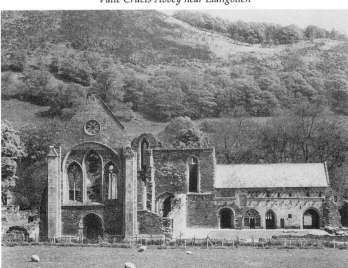

LLANGOLLEN TO REJOIN ODP TREVOR ROCKS

From the town cross the bridge over the Dee and turn right. At the corner where a taxidermist displays his craft turn left up Wharf Hill. Bear right

MAP 13/1

to cross the canal to join the signed tarmac path opposite and follow this northwards for 1/2 mile passing school, houses and over other tracks and through kissing gates until you reach the open hillside.

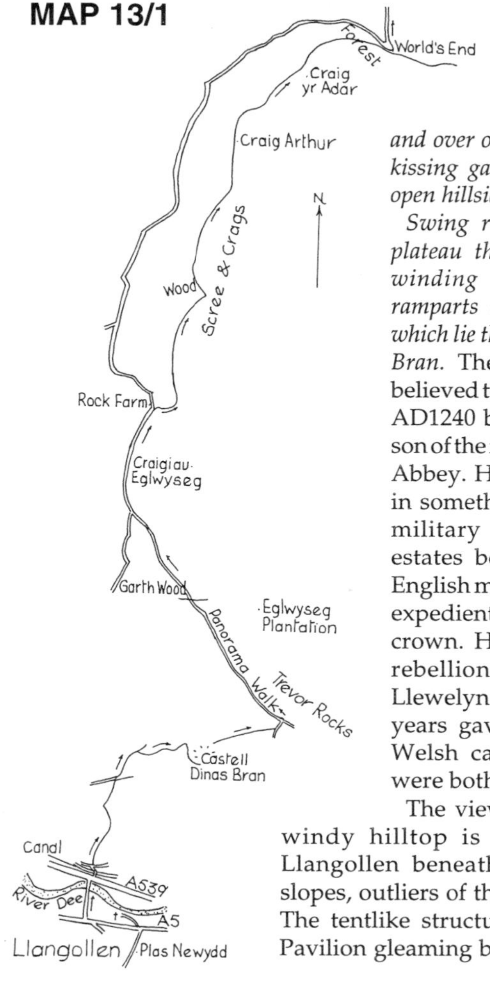

Swing right to cross a grassy plateau then climb steeply on a winding path to the southern ramparts of the hill fort, within which lie the ruins of Castell Dinas Bran. The mediaeval castle is believed to have been built about AD1240 by Gruffyd ap Madog son of the founder of Valle Crucis Abbey. He seems to have been in something of a political and military cleft stick since his estates bordered those of the English marcher lords making it expedient to show loyalty to the crown. He did not join in the rebellion led by Davydd ap Llewelyn in 1244 but in later years gave his support to the Welsh cause. Father and son were both buried in the abbey.

The view from this high and windy hilltop is superb. Below lies Llangollen beneath the steep forested slopes, outliers of the Berwyn mountains. The tentlike structure of the new Royal Pavilion gleaming brilliant white is easily

183

Stumpy ruins of Castell Dinas Bran

picked out on the western edge of the town. To the east the Dee flows through the long vale of Llangollen passing under Telford's great aqueduct, the many pillared railway viaduct and the new still white concrete bridge that carries the modern road. To the north the great limestone stepped cliffs stretch for miles with Trevor Rocks immediately behind Dinas Bran.

Descend by the waymarked path which at first heads south then swings to the north-east falling sharply to meet and cross a stile found just beyond a clump of gorse. Turn left to meet the road to rejoin the route of the ODP under Trevor Rocks.

TREVOR ROCKS TO WORLD'S END

Turn left and follow the single track road for 1½ miles as it veers from north-west to north shadowing the high cliffs of Trevor Rocks and Creigiau Eglwyseg. Just before Rock Cottage is met the ODP is signed off right through a metal gateway.

There now follows a 2 mile passage under the crags and across the scree slopes of the western scarp of Eglwyseg Mountain. Perhaps the best of the ODP in the Llangollen area, with fine airy views down

Trevor Rocks and the Panorama Walk from Castell Dinas Bran

to the remote farms dotted about the lower slopes. The waymarked path runs higher than the road, never far from it, but it is not easily regained until World's End is reached. If cursed with bad weather or very poor visibility walkers may opt to remain with the road.

From the gateway head towards the facing scree slopes on a wide track then curving left over a (possibly) dry stream bed. Soon the slate roofed, white house of Bryn Goleu is passed to your left, with peacocks in its small courtyard: how strange it seems in this environment.

The fenceline is left as the path terraces the slopes under the cliffs fulfilling the promise of fine views from a narrow but clear path that runs across the scree with any uncertainties resolved by the regular waymarks.

Craig Arthur is seen well ahead as the path falls a little to cross a stream just above a patch of woodland with the farm of Plas Yn Eglwyseg seen below at the junction of two lanes.

Continue northwards on a narrow but clear tread under "the awesome white cliffs" as some of the poetic visitors to the Ladies of Llangollen might have been moved to call them. The ODP is now following a line about 150 yards above the fence to the left. The up to now clear path briefly all but disappears but is quickly picked up again beyond a stream to continue over the scree. The towering iced cake shaped Craig Arthur becoming increasingly dominant.

After rounding the slopes under Craig Arthur the ODP gradually edges towards the fence line. As the woodland seen away to your left begins to fall back go half left at a Y-junction descending along the fence line.

Remain with the fence to meet woodland and continue still with the fence to your left, soon to cross a ladder stile. From here go forward through old woodland now cleared but liable to be replanted, soon following a wider track. Below to the left there is a glimpse of the old Manor House, recently restored. The ODP descends towards the conifer plantation to cross a stile thence forward on a dark but wide track. At an indistinct Y-junction take the right, ie. forward track, descending gently and running parallel with the road, which is met just short of a hairpin bend at World's End.

WORLD'S END TO PEN-Y-STRYT

Turn right with the road which soon splashes through a ford and continue passing an old lime kiln and with a colourful view down the valley. In ½ mile the road leaves the forested area, remain with it for a further ¾ mile as it makes its narrow way through high rolling moorland stretching, or so it seems to infinity.

When the mist wraithes the forest in a cobwebby shroud and the clouds hang low over the black peaty carpet of heather there is little reason to wonder why it came to be called World's End.

At last when you begin to think you have missed the turn the ODP is signed off on the left. The once notorious way over the moor has been greatly improved with board walks over the wetter patches, and generously waymarked in the eroded areas. The narrowing (but still clear) path rises north-westerly to meet the forest boundary in ¾ mile.

Cross into the forest by a "Welcome to Llandegla Forest" sign erected by the Shotton Paper Company which has improved the rights of way and provided waymarked circular walks. These and the ODP are indicated on the board.

Go forward with the ODP continuing its north-westerly course for 1¼ miles, a straightforward well signed route despite the occasional twist and turn.

After level walking on a broad track, cross a forest road beyond which the ODP begins a gentle descent to cross a further forest road. The path narrows with wet patches eased by a carpet of forest bark or bridging. A long steady fall opens out to a slightly more open area at a T-junction of paths. Cross a plank bridge over a stream (notice proclaims this to be "Aqueduct Wrexham

MAP 13/2

Water") and turn left to follow it for 60 yards. Turn right on a narrow falling path. In just over 100 yards cross three bridges in quick succession linked by a stepped path. Beyond the third bridge turn left and continue the descent to cross a further forest road and onward with more open landscape seen ahead and a deep ravine to your left.

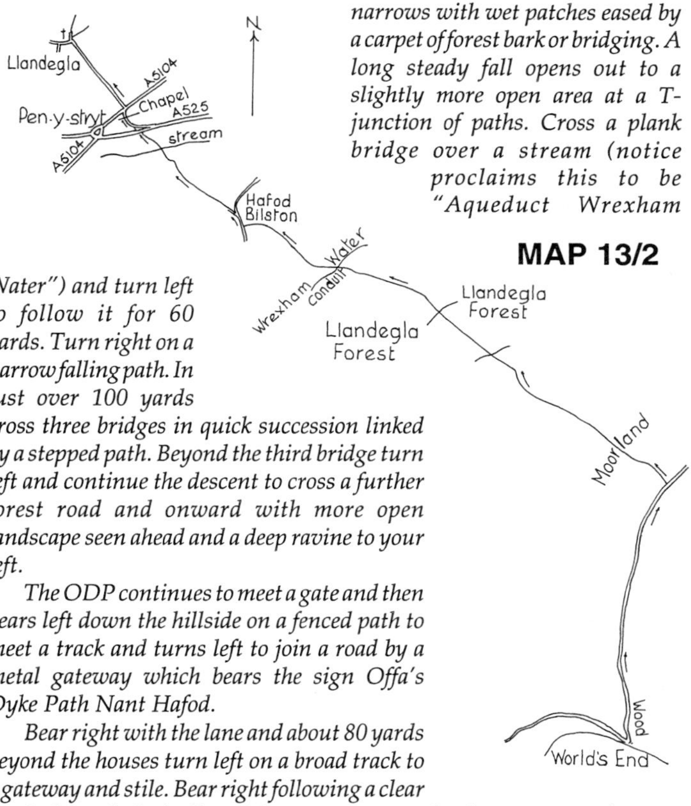

The ODP continues to meet a gate and then bears left down the hillside on a fenced path to meet a track and turns left to join a road by a metal gateway which bears the sign Offa's Dyke Path Nant Hafod.

Bear right with the lane and about 80 yards beyond the houses turn left on a broad track to a gateway and stile. Bear right following a clear track along the hedgeline rising to meet a gate by the remnants of a stone wall and stile. Go forward following the fence line to your left, to descend over a large field towards power lines. At the pylon turn left over a stile then slightly diagonally right over field and a stream to a stile, then up the hillside to meet a road (A525). (Sign at bridge announces camping at Llyn Rhys Farm.)

Turn left with the road and shortly right on a hedged and fenced path between houses to meet a lane. Turn left curving with the lane to meet the main road (A5104 signed Chester right) by the old chapel at Pen-y-stryt.

14: Pen-y-stryt to Bwlch Penbarra

MAPS: 1:25,000 Pathfinder   788 (SJ 05/15)
                                   772 (SJ 06/16) (small section)
        1:50,000 Landranger   116 Denbigh & Colwyn Bay

FACILITIES: Shops, refreshments and accommodation at Pen-y-stryt/
        Llandegla. Accommodation possibilities Clwyd Gate and off route:
        Ruthin area etc.

PARKING FOR ROUND WALKS: Bwlch Penbarra.

MILEAGE CHART:
Pen-y-stryt to Clwyd Gate   6
Clwyd Gate to Bwlch Penbarra   2¹/₂

Total   8¹/₂

The official route is followed throughout.

This section embarks on the crossing of the Clwydian Hills described by some walkers as the hardest part of the Offa's Dyke Path. Not that this is particularly difficult terrain. The paths are for the most part clear on the ground and whilst there is some "switchback" walking with the highest point found on Moel Fammau (next chapter) at 1,818 feet the gradients are not too demanding. Circumstances alter cases and taking in the full crossing from Llandegla to Bodfari will test walkers' stamina the more so on a blustery day or when temperatures are high. The route description has therefore been split into almost equal sections to which is added the further suggestion that in making individual itineraries a start from Clwyd Gate may be helpful. In this connection the route from Llangollen might be extended to that point making a 14¹/₂ mile day followed by an 11¹/₄ mile crossing of the higher hills. Scenically this has much to commend it but it might be advisable to book accommodation in advance (bed and breakfast signs were in evidence on route at Bwlch Uchaf to the east of Clwyd Gate).

The closing chapters of this book concern themselves almost entirely with the crossing of the hills but walkers including a general tour of the area are referred to the Useful Information section. As the ODP progresses over the hills the views to the west look over the Vale of Clwyd, which Daniel Defoe, no lover of mountains, found entirely to his taste with an exuberant description of the richness of its agriculture.

Ruthin is a pleasant old town associated with the marcher lordship of the de Grey family who developed it as a market and centre of the weaving industry.

Denbigh has a fine castle dating from 1282 which was later the home of the Myddletons. The cathedral at St Asaph is well worth a visit, particularly for the fine old books on display which include what is probably the earliest book of common prayer in Welsh, dated 1586, and a breeches bible of 1597.

Further north Rhuddlan Castle built with a dock so that it could be supplied from the sea via the canalised Clwyd River presents a picture of great strength within its deep moat. It was here that Edward I presented his infant son to the Welsh people as the prince that could speak no English - he neglected to say that he couldn't speak any Welsh either. Unhappily what Henry VIII did for the monasteries, Cromwell did for many a fine castle and Rhuddlan was greatly reduced following the Civil War when it was garrisoned for the Royalist cause.

PEN-Y-STRYT TO CLWYD GATE

On meeting the main road, the A5104, cross by the old chapel and continue to Llandegla with a village store and St Teclas church at the end of the street.

The village derives its name from the eighth century saint, Tegla (or Thecla), and has a well dedicated to her. The Welsh connection seems obscure since she was a nun of the Benedictine order at Wimbourne in Dorset who travelled to the continent to aid Boniface's missionary work and later became head of a German convent.

Leave the village road as it curves to the left and go forward on a track which runs between the church and the Old Rectory. After passing a Welsh Water installation maintain your direction over a long field with hedge and stream to your left. At the end of the field turn left over a footbridge and bear

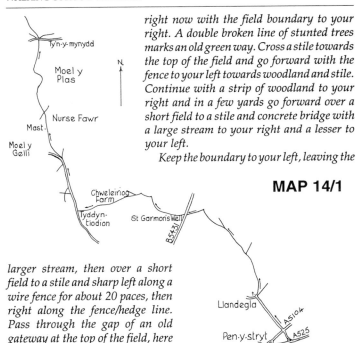

right now with the field boundary to your right. A double broken line of stunted trees marks an old green way. Cross a stile towards the top of the field and go forward with the fence to your left towards woodland and stile. Continue with a strip of woodland to your right and in a few yards go forward over a short field to a stile and concrete bridge with a large stream to your right and a lesser to your left.

Keep the boundary to your left, leaving the

MAP 14/1

larger stream, then over a short field to a stile and sharp left along a wire fence for about 20 paces, then right along the fence/hedge line. Pass through the gap of an old gateway at the top of the field, here turn left up a hedged track passing a rocky outcrop to meet a narrow road, the B5431.

Cross the lane to take the farm track announced by the sign "Chweleiriog" and remain with it for about 750 yards.

Another well dedicated to a saint is noted on the map - St Garmon - otherwise known as Germanus. There have been at least two saints of this name with Welsh connections. Germanus of Auxerre a fifth-century bishop who twice visited Britain to rebuff the perceived heretical teachings of the monk Pelagius who denounced the concept of original sin and preached the gospel of free will. Geoffrey of Monmouth in his *History of the Kings of Britain* mentions the visitation of Germanus with Lupus and refers to their working of many miracles. Another Germanus of the same era, also French born, had an ecclesiastical career which encompassed a sojourn in Ireland with its patron saint, Patrick, and residence in Welsh monasteries.

The track swings to the right after a cattle grid, then bears left after crossing a stream. When the farm at Chweleiriog comes into view leave the track (about 250 yards short of the farm and just beyond a small clump of trees passed on your right) turning left, at first with the boundary to your left, climbing gently to the top of the field.

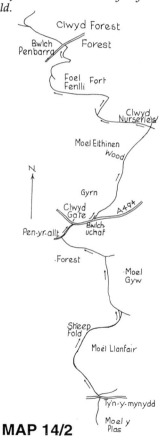

Beyond the stile go slightly diagonally left and on to cross the next field (very slightly right with a broken boundary of trees to your left). From the next stile bear left along the field edge to a stile where go ahead towards farm buildings which are passed to your left, to meet a stile and turn right on a narrow lane. Follow the lane northwards for 800 yards. The road which dips to meet a forested area should be abandoned as it bends to the left.

The hill walking proper begins from this point with views in abundance over a delightful countryside of heather covered moorland, high pastures, tumbling streams, broadleaved and conifer woods, the multicoloured fields of the Vale and onward to the mighty mountains of Snowdonia.

Go towards the forest and as the way divides at a Y-junction bear half left, signed Moel y Plas. Head up the hillside on the good track with the plantations of Nurse Fawr on your right, passing a wireless mast to your left as the ODP continues along the fence line.

The path over a grassy plateau

MAP 14/2

soon dips and by a gate with a view to Llyn Gweryd, bear slightly diagonally left, falling then rising to a gateway and ladder stile. Beyond the stile climb steeply over grass to the fence seen on the skyline. At the fence bear right and in 80 yards turn left over a stile and half right cutting off the angle of a fenced area of moorland. As you meet the fence bear left.

To your right beyond the enclosed heather rises the green topped Moel y Plas while to your left the wild moorland plunges away with a long view down the valley.

There is a clear path running along the fence line initially with only a gentle rise and fall. As the road ahead comes into view the path veers away a little from the fenceline to descend by a stepped path then on to reach a track just to the west of the farm at Ty'n-y-mynydd.

Turn left with the track and in a few yards right over a stile and head along the fence. To your right is Moel Llech then Moel Llanfair and to the left a view over the Vale of Clwyd with Ruthin seen in the north-west. The good, broad track terraces the hillside - green pastures in contrast with the heather covering of Moel Gyw.

A little under ¾ mile after joining the track, with sheepfolds seen below left, a metal gateway and stile are met. Here turn sharp right with the track as it climbs steadily along the northern flanks of Moel Llanfair.

In ¼ mile, near the top of the rise, turn left over a stile and go forward soon to join a path coming in from the right. Turn left with this as it follows the heather clad slopes of Moel Gyw - 1,532 feet. As you advance the long woodland of Coed Plas-y-nant is seen to your left and northward beyond Bwlch-y-parc the hills of Gyrn and Moel Eithinen.

The ODP descends to the fenceline with woodland to your left to meet a stile. From here bear half left climbing over a small hillock with Coed Plas-y-nant to your left. Continue, a little north of west, on a grassy tread to meet a stile beyond which bear very slight right over a field to meet a farm lane at Pen-yr-allt.

Turn right with the lane and follow this for 300 yards to meet the A494 by the Clwyd Gate Inn and Motel. To the left, in 1½ miles is the village of Llanbedr-Dyffryn-Clwyd and then Ruthin (3¼ miles). Both have accommodation possibilities with taxis available at Ruthin and a telephone box at Clwyd Gate. Accommodation may also be found nearer at hand at Clwyd Gate and Bwlch-uchaf.

CLWYD GATE TO BWLCH PENBARRA

Turn right and follow the main road for just over 300 yards leaving it in favour of the bridleway signed on the left. When the track divides take the right fork, passing houses to climb steadily along the eastern slopes of Gyrn - 1,260 feet. When the track again divides at a Y-junction take the forward (left) option, moving away from the hedgeline as you continue north-east with the gorse fringed, gated and cattle gridded bridleway.

About ¹/₂ mile after leaving the A494 there is a further division of the way met just before a patch of woodland, another Y-junction. Take the upper climbing path (ie. left) which soon makes a slight descent to a gateway and stile to cross the lower end of the plantation. Beyond this the bridleway maintains the same direction for just over ¹/₄ mile, with a broken stone wall to your right and soon passing Moel-eithinen Farm, with the hill from which it takes its name rising to over 1,420 feet on your left.

On meeting a gateway, with the farm at Fron-heulog seen on the hillside ahead turn left (westwards), following the line of a drystone wall to pass the conifer plantations of Clwyd Nurseries to your right and the probability of seeing hares in the fields to your left.

There is much folklore associated with these creatures, who unlike rabbits do not provide the comparative safety of a burrow for their offspring but somehow survive in a modest scrape in the ground. It was claimed that hares annually changed sex, that witches took on their form when seeking a disguise and if one crossed your path ill fortune would surely follow. Shakespeare refers to their supposed melancholia while the wild boxing antics in the March mating season has provided the language with a useful simile for madness.

After passing the woodland a stile is crossed and the ODP continues climbing, with the fence on the left, heading towards the right of twin pointed hillocks. At the top of the field bear right along the fence to a stile, now with the steep heather covered slopes of Foel Fenlli blocking your forward view.

Descend with the fenceline to your left and conifers to your right to Bwlch Crug-glas. At one time the ODP went directly over the 1,676-foot summit with its egg shaped hill fort. A legend claims that in the fifth century the site was occupied by an oppressive chieftain whose settlement was destroyed in a great and mysterious fire following an encounter with the saintly Germanus. A pity to ruin a good story but it might be supposed that the wooden huts of the time would have been at risk from cooking fires while the exposed position would have rendered a bolt from the blue a natural hazard without divine intervention.

Initially the path seems determined to head directly over the stronghold. Go forward slightly right up the eastern slopes of the hill on a winding path through heather and bilberry. In about 300 yards a waymark directs you left on a narrow but clear path that runs westward under the summit with views over the Vale of Clwyd towards Ruthin.

A slight rise heads towards a little ridge as you round the hillside but before this is reached bear left at a marker post descending to follow a grassy path with level walking along the lower banks beneath the western summit.

As you reach the northern edge there is a fine view over the pass, the well trodden tracks which lead to the summit of the range, Moel Fammu, seen above the dark green of the Clwyd Forest. The ODP is signed off half left and then almost immediately curves right to descend steadily eastwards. A final serpentine twist brings you to the road at Bwlch Penbarra with its car park and the large information board of the Moel Fammau Country Park which encompasses over 20,000 acres.

The village of Llanbedr-Dyffryn-Clwyd lies to the left and can be reached in just over a mile by way of a steep descending winding road with Ruthin a further $1^1/2$ miles via the A494.

15: Mother of the Mountains
Bwlch Penbarra to Bodfari

MAPS:	1:25,000 Pathfinder	772 (SJ 06/16)
		755 (SJ 07/17) (minute portion)
	1:50,000 Landranger	116 Denbigh & Colwyn Bay

FACILITIES: Shops, refreshments and accommodation on route at Bodfari. Off route at Ruthin and Llanbedr-Dyffryn-Clwyd.

PARKING FOR ROUND WALKS: Bwlch Penbarra, the minor roads under Moel Arthur and to the south-east of Penycloddiau and some informal parking seems to be used on the track near Nant Coed-y-mynydd. Layby, A541 Bodfari.

MILEAGE CHART:

Bwlch Penbarra to foot of Moel Arthur	4$\frac{1}{4}$
Moel Arthur to Bodfari	4$\frac{1}{2}$
Total	8$\frac{3}{4}$

The section follows the official route throughout.

May the gods of good weather be with you blessing your day with blue skies, billowing white clouds and light cooling breezes, for this crossing of the high moorlands of the Moel Fammau Country Park deserves to be enjoyed to the full. The country park covers over 20,000 acres with extensive views that encompass the mountains of Snowdonia, the Vale of Clwyd, the estuary of the Dee and Liverpool Bay. It is said that on the clearest of days (how rare they are) the Isle of Man, the Lake District mountains and the Blackpool Tower can be picked out. The hill top dwellers found a home here up to 2,000 years ago. Foel Fenlli has already been skirted, the hill top fort of Moel y Gaer is soon seen to the west, with Moel Arthur and Penycloddiau encountered as the walk progresses.

Heather carpets much of the highest ground, black in winter, slowly greening as summer moves on apace until it bursts forth into the purple glory of August. Here in summer the piping call of the

The base of the now fallen Jubilee Tower, Moel Fammau

curlew is heard and the red grouse flies fast and low over the hills in a sudden startled commotion that betrays its otherwise unsuspected presence. On the eastern slopes rising almost to the summit of Moel Fammau is the Forestry Commission's Clwyd Forest with a picnic site and woodland paths open to walkers.

It was in 1810 that thousands of people trekked up to the summit for the dedication of the tall tower being built to honour the fiftieth year of the reign of George III. Sadly in the following year his son was appointed regent for the rest of his reign (to 1820) as the madness which had periodically afflicted him over the years took final command of his reason. The tower completed in 1812 stood 115 feet high and for fifty years was a landmark which dominated a wide area of the countryside. But it was to suffer the fate of many such column and its own jubilee was marked in disastrous fashion when the autumn gales of 1862 brought all but the 15 feet high base crashing to the ground. It was never rebuilt but some restoration work in 1970 brought back some order and increased the viewer's interest in the landscape with identifying plaques.

BWLCH PENBARRA TO MOEL ARTHUR

Walkers who join the route at the top of the pass start with a bonus if they have arrived by car for they have already reached the 1,500 feet contour with only a modest 320 feet to be added in the next 1³/₄ miles to reach the topmost summit of the range.

A toposcope by the car park identifies the notable buildings of Ruthin including the Old Court House of 1400, Ruthin School founded 1248 and the church of 1248. The wider landscape is not neglected, the distant peaks in the western arc include the Arran Hills, Cader Idris 2,927 feet, Arenig Fawr, Snowdon 3,560 feet - the highest mountain in England and Wales, Tryfan 3,010 feet, and the Carneddu. Eastward views are denied until the summit of Moel Fammau is reached.

The paths to the Jubilee Tower are well worn, erosion has become a problem but has been eased by the closing of some subsidiary paths.

From the car park go forward to the metal gateway to take the wide track which winds up the hillside. In a few yards the way divides, ignore the right fork and remain with the wider track which terraces the hillside with the promised views to Ruthin and the distant mountain ranges. Nearer at hand the fields of the Vale of Clwyd are laid out in chequer-board fashion with sheep grazing the lower slopes like an armada of white sailed yachts becalmed upon a sea of green.

There are several paths

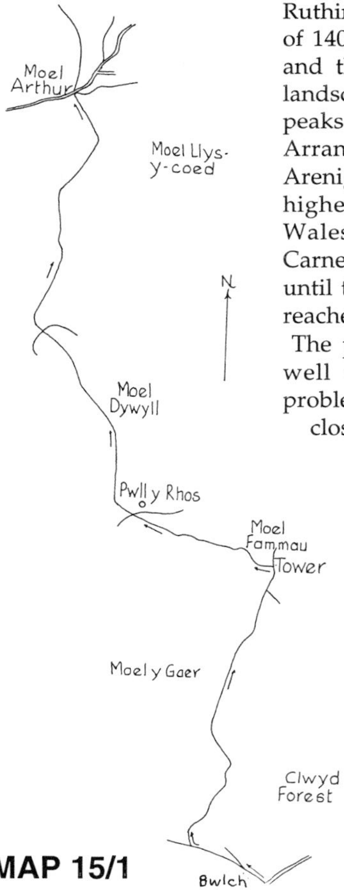

MAP 15/1

Moel Arthur
Moel Llys-y-coed
N
Moel Dywyll
Pwll y Rhos
Moel Fammau
Tower
Moel y Gaer
Clwyd Forest
Bwlch

A network of well worn tracks leads to the summit of Moel Fammau

which leave the main route but the waymarking will quickly resolve any uncertainties. The mountains of Snowdonia become more prominent as progress is made and the hill fort of Moel y Gaer will be seen forward left. The summit of Moel Fammau with the substantial stump of the celebratory tower comes into view with the track taking a clear but winding course with the forest boundary edging closer as the final ascent is made.

After nearly 300 years the base of the once great tower appears more like an oversized and long abandoned pill box than a kingly tribute. It might be supposed if the tower had honoured a Wellington or a Nelson greater efforts might have been made to maintain its place on the skyline. There are no battle honours to be listed at the foot of the column but the long reign of George III was as eventful as most including the American War of Independence and conflict with France and Spain. It was an age which produced a remarkable list of literary achievement which ranged widely over the fields of scholarship, romanticism, comedy, eloquence, politics, mysticism, satire, drama and poetry with writers as diverse as Lawrence

Sterne, Thomas Gray, Horace Walpole, Oliver Goldsmith, Jonathan Swift, Edward Gibbon, Edmund Burke, Sheridan, Johnson and Boswell, Fanny Burney and Jane Austen, Blake, Cowper, Crabbe, Burns, Gilbert White the Hampshire naturalist and clergyman, Wordsworth, Sir Walter Scott and Lord Byron. The cast list of actors on the political stage included Grenville, Pitt-father and son, Lord North, Rockingham, Canning, Castlereagh, John Wilkes and Spencer Percival the only British prime minister to be assassinated while in office. The observation platform provided by the stump is enhanced by the comprehensive set of toposcopes at the angle of each wall. To the east as the forest falls away the Dee is seen clearly beyond the green fields and further points may include Liverpool Pierhead 20 miles, the Merseyside refinery at Stanlow and nearer at hand the prominent quarry face of Cefn Mawr. The northern arc features Denbigh, Liverpool Bay, and Crosby. The southern view is more constricted as it looks over the Clwyd Forest to Foel Fenlli and the inevitable wireless mast, while the western view to the ring of far away mountains has already been described.

From the tower there is a change of direction as the ODP heads north-west with the path soon descending, later steeply, with a stone wall to your right and the gleam of Pwll y Rhos ahead. The pool is seen beyond the wall as you dip to a crossing path before rising to Moel Dywyll where the cairn is passed to your left.

The ODP continues to shadow the wall with a stretch of level walking and a view ahead to Moel Llys-y-coed and the reservoir at Garth to the east.

The path climbs again before falling to meet a wide, rough track and a Moel Fammau Park board and finger posts. Continue over the track signed Moel Llys-y-coed climbing with the remains of the stone wall to your right. As you reach the top of a short rise bear right along the wall and right again on a good climbing track with a wireless mast seen ahead. In the far distance a long line of houses marks the distant coastal strip and the almost imperceptible horizon where the slate blue sea meets the sky.

At the top of Moel Llys-y-coed bear right along the boundary for a while with the smooth monkish tonsure-like head of Moel Arthur seen to the north. After a short level stretch the ODP descends through heather and bilberry. As you approach the end of the heather the path swings sharp left, partly stepped to ease the steep descent to the road and car park beneath Moel Arthur.

MOEL ARTHUR TO BODFARI.

This narrow pass, like Bwlch Penbarra, was one of the mountain roads taken by the drovers on the long trek through Wales to the markets and lusher pastures across the border. A few miles to the east lies Mold, once the county town of Flintshire. It was near here that a surprising battle was fought and won, not primarily by force of arms but by faith and a great roar from the lusty throats of the British. The story dates back to the visit to Britain in AD429 of Germanus, Bishop of Auxerre who had been invited to rebuff the spread of the supposed heretical teachings of the monk Pelagius. After his successful verbal defeat of Pelagius's adherents in a lively debate near St Albans, the Bishop's further help was sought by the British against raiding parties of Picts and Saxons on the border country

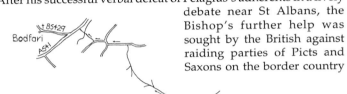

MAP 15/2

which we now called Clwyd. He urged them to put on a bold face and have faith and baptised those who felt ready to accept the tenets of Christianity.

At the time of the great festival of Easter Germanus assembled his forces in a narrow mountain valley and lying hidden, quietly awaited the close approach of the foe. At a signal the British rose up and as one man gave three mighty cries of Alleluia which reverberated off the mountain walls like the thunder of doomsday. The effect on the morale of the invaders was devastating and they turned and fled. The site of the battle was called Maes Garmon and the triumph, the Alleluia Victory.

Turn right with the road and in a short distance (towards the end of the car park area) go through a kissing gate taking the path which winds steeply up the hillside with the hill fort of Moel Arthur well to your left.

The view opens out to reveal the sea, the Wirral Peninsular, the Dee and the Mersey.

Continue with the fence line to your right. As you come roughly level with the northern side of the fort (some distance away) the ODP deserts the fence and bears half left over the heather moorland on a good track which provides views towards Denbigh and the Vale of Clwyd with the mountains of Snowdonia again providing the distant backdrop.

A gentle descent to the north-west steepens with the hill fort of Penycloddiau seen ahead. As the heather comes to an end cross a stile set in the fenceline and go forward over pasture with woods seen rising from the valley ahead. Beyond a further stile descend slightly diagonally left towards woodland. Cross a stile by a small stream and go ahead through the trees soon to meet a minor road and turn right.

In a short distance bear left into the car park and through a gateway with a sign which announces the Forestry Commissions's Clwyd Forest, Wangwyfan Wood. Go ahead on the broad track which immediately divides. Take the rising right fork for a few yards, turn right, then forward on a narrower path under conifers with the fence to your right.

Keep with the rising path on the inside edge of the wood for ½ mile before emerging into a more open area with further views over the Vale - recent plantings may soon obscure this. Cross a stile and head up the hillside with the fence to your left to meet in about 200 yards a small stone cairn and waymark.

The ODP used to follow the western ramparts of the Penycloddiau hill fort but now takes the broad track through the centre to the summit cairn with wide views in all directions.

From the cairn dip and rise over the bank and bear right for a few yards before turning left over the four ramparts that guarded the northern approaches.

Forest

Moel
Arthur

A short period of level walking leads to a descent on a clear grassy path to meet a stile from which go very slightly diagonally right on a fainter path.

By the stile there is a slate memorial to Arthur Roberts MBE of Offa's Ramblers Holidays. The stile too bears his initials and the dates 1905-1991, a nice tribute to one who loved the hills.

Continue over a minor hillock to meet a cairn where bear left along the crest of the hill initially in the direction of the TV mast. The good, springy grass path veers away to the north-west still on the hilltop before descending over pasture. The path dips half right on a slightly narrower track with the farm of Nant Coed-y-mynydd seen ahead and an old stone wall poking through the bracken to your right.

The ODP meets a crossing path by a metal gate/stile where turn right and in a few yards left on a rough track beyond a further gateway and stile.

The track is followed westwards as it curves down the hillside between ancient walls. Continue beyond a gateway and stile passing derelict farm buildings, with the ODP briefly shaded by trees, to a further gateway/stile. The track now passes under the steeply banked hillside with purple spears of foxglove thrusting through the green summer bracken.

The path falls to Ty Newydd where an innovative piece of farmyard plumbing may be seen as you cross a streamlet: a length of guttering conducts the spring water to a churn, where a hose has been connected to provide water to the barns below.

Shortly cross a stream and in 40 yards leave the main track to turn sharp left on a grassy bridleway which terraces the hillside with Bodfari's church appearing through the trees and the distant sea seen ahead.

About ½ mile after joining the bridleway keep an eye open for the waymark that directs ODP walkers to bear half left on a lesser path to the fence line which is followed to your left to meet a metal gateway and stile.

Bear left over the stile and resume your forward direction over rough grassland now with the church tower seen more clearly. The indistinct path falls gently and in about 200 yards is waymarked half left towards the fence line and stile. Beyond the stile bear half right to a further stile from which cross the short end of a field, over a stile and then onward with a fence to your right. Beyond the next stile keep with the fence and in 100 yards bear half left over the field to meet a stile and turn right on a metalled lane for a few yards by a house called Grove Goch.

Turn left down a lane to meet a T-junction and bear right. In a few yards turn left on a lane and as it bends to the left after passing a large house, turn right through an iron kissing gate. Follow the path with the fence to your left to cross the fast flowing River Wheeler by a footbridge thence over a short field to meet the main road (A541) opposite the Spar Grocers at Bodfari. (The church which has been in sight for some time lies a little to the west.)

16: The Last Lap
Bodfari to Prestatyn

MAPS: 1:25,000 Pathfinder   755 (SJ 07/17)
                                    737 (SJ 08/18)
         1:50,000 Landranger   116 Denbigh & Colwyn Bay

FACILITIES: Shops, accommodation and refreshments at Bodfari and
    Prestatyn. Bed and breakfast Tremeirchion and Rhuallt area and
    bunkhouse.

MILEAGE CHART:
Bodfari to Rhuallt   4¼
Rhuallt to Prestatyn Station   7¼

Total   11½

The section follows the official route throughout.

The closing miles of the ODP follow quiet lanes and field paths with
the finale a passage along the inland cliffs that looks down to the golf
courses and roof tops of the coastal strip and beyond to long sandy
beaches and the Irish Sea. The Clwydian Hills although lessening in
height, continue towards Rhuallt and the now familiar view to the
outlines of Snowdonia appears at intervals. The narrowing gap to
the once distant sea may give rise to a hearty cheer as it signals a
pilgrimage nearly completed. Celebration may take another form
for on this last stage we passed and in turn were passed by a small
group who had followed the Offa's Dyke Path northwards over a
period of two years. They carried with them a bottle of champagne
with which to toast their achievement at journey's end. The cork
was duly popped, not on the North Wales shore but 5 miles inland
amidst the bracken of the slopes above Rhuallt - we never saw them
again - but perhaps they had a second celebratory drink at Prestatyn.

BODFARI TO RHUALLT

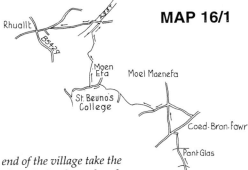

MAP 16/1

Bodfari church with its post office, shop and Dinorben Arms Inn of 1640 lies a little to the west of the point where the ODP crosses the A541. *If start-ing from the western end of the village take the minor road eastwards from St Stephens church (note the neat war memorial with a marching soldier). A path to be found on the left will bring you to the small group of houses and further shops at the point where the ODP meets the main road.*

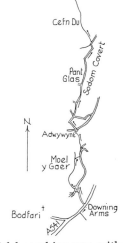

Picking up the route from the south, turn right along the A541 and follow this as far as the Downing Arms. I am not sure what the local association is; the naturalist and travel writer Thomas Pennant came from Downing not so very far away but the connection may be with the titled family of that name. The first baronet, Sir George Downing fought for the Parliamentary cause in the Civil War of 1642-1651 and later followed a diplomatic career under Cromwell and after the restoration of the monarchy for Charles II. Downing built the row of terraced houses off Whitehall which bears his name, with number 10 arguably the most famous address in the capital without the security of tenure afforded by the royal palaces. It has been the official residence of successive prime ministers from 1731 when Sir Robert Walpole held the office. The third baronet, also Sir George, who died in 1717 bequeathed his estate to found Downing College, Cambridge.

Opposite the Downing Arms, take the narrow, metalled lane which climbs steeply to meet a road junction in 300 yards. Here turn left and in 20 paces right over a stile bearing slight diagonally right over the hillside passing a small plantation of broadleafed trees to your right. The path gives views of the Vale of Clwyd and back to Moel y Parc (1,306 feet) and its wireless mast. Beyond the stile found near the corner of the field follow the fence line with Moel y Gaer and its fort rising to your left.

As you pass a small group of Scots pines bear left and after passing an old quarry cross a stile, now heading northwards under the eastern slopes of Moel y Gaer. The path soon dips to meet a fence and in a short distance cross a stile and track to bear half right over a field to meet and turn left on a lane.

The lane soon divides, take the left rising fork, and leave it by the stile found just short of the gate carrying the legend Moel y Gaer. Cross the field with the fence to your left with a great exuberant splash of flaming yellow gorse seen on the hillside above the white houses of the little hamlet of Adwywynt. Cross further fields to meet the lane and turn right, then left at road junction. Follow the climbing road northwards for ¾ mile with views to the west which include St Asaph and the 200 feet spire of the "marble church" at Bodelwyddan, built in the 1850s as a memorial to Sir Willoughby de Broke.

Sodom Covert with some fine Scots pines is to your right and later the white painted slate roofed house at Pant Glas is passed on the left under tumulus topped slopes. Towards the end of the woodland, leave the road as it curves to the right. (A bunk house is signed off left at this point.)

Take the northward path beyond the stile with the fenceline to your left and plantation to your right. Beyond a stile in a broken boundary continue climbing with further plantations on your right to meet a stile where continue along the fenceline with improving views of the mountains in the west. Head over a short field to a stile to cross the summit of Cefn Du and as the fence you have been following veers to the left, go half right over the field (your distant landmark the western end of Coed Bron-fawr). No visible path here but a waymarked post will keep you in the right direction to meet the stile set in a wire fence.

From the stile bear half left with a further marker post as you descend towards the road. Beyond a gateway and stile (bunk house signed left here) go forward to meet a minor road and follow this northwards for nearly ½ mile. Pass under power lines at a road junction, the derelict farm house that was Pant Glas and as the road bends left the woodland of Coed-Bron-fawr.

At a road junction (signed Rhuallt right and Tremeirchion left) turn left and then very shortly right following a minor road for ¹/₄ mile. As you reach further power lines just before a road junction, turn left on a hedged green lane generously decorated with wild flowers in season.

This bridleway can be followed to St Beunos, but in 300 yards the ODP leaves it by a stile found on the right to head north-west over the lower slopes of Moel Maenefa. The choice of route clearly dictated by the fine westward prospect.

From the stile head half left over the field to meet a further stile from which maintain your direction making for a pair of trees and a marker post. From here there is an improved view to the coast and the many patterned still hedged fields of the Vale broken by numerous woods and dingles.

Now head slightly diagonally right descending through gorse on a widening path to meet a stile and over a further field to rejoin the bridleway. Turn right with the bridleway which falls sharply to meet a lane by a house called Benarth.

Bear left with the lane still descending in the direction of (but not to) St Beuno's College. In 200 yards turn right over a stile.

Some changes to the ODP have been made following the improvements to the A55 trunk road and the route to Rhuallt as described may be subject to further alteration. This is unlikely to cause walkers any great problem since such diversions are invariably very well waymarked.

From the stile cross the field making for the stile found a little below the buildings of Maen Efa. Go forward on the permissive path towards a line of trees to descend by steps. Thence half left over a field to meet stile set in the hedgerow and go ahead with the fence a little to your right to meet and cross a stile by a metal gateway. Continue to a further stile and on to the top of the field where turn right along the fence with the A55 seen below in the deep cutting to your left.

In 200 yards turn left over the footbridge to join the lane which descends to Rhuallt - Blue Lion Inn and Smithy Arms.

RHUALLT TO PRESTATYN

For the traveller following the ODP hill forts have been an obvious indication of pre-historic man's presence. References on the map to caves may have been noted from time to time, some of which have yielded proof of man's occupancy before they were abandoned in favour of the wider community life of the defended camps. One such, Cae-Gwyn near Tremeirchion revealed the remains of a number of animals long extinct from this country, lion, rhinocerous, hyenas as well as deer and tools dating back perhaps 25,000 years. The line of a Roman road ran eastwards towards Rhuallt. On Gop Hill near Trelawynd, about a mile to the east of the ODP a large and ancient cairn marks the summit. Animal remains have been found in nearby caves together with human skeletons of the Neolithic period.

From Rhuallt village take the right fork passing the Smithy Arms to follow the lane for ¼ mile, passing Hendre Sian on your left. Turn right over a stile to climb steeply through woodland with an old stone wall on your right. The trees thin as the ODP maintains a north-easterly direction beyond a stile again with the wall to your right and open fields beyond. The extensive forested area of Coed Cwm lies to your left.

As you reach the edge of a conifer plantation bear right with the fence to your left to meet a stile. Go forward crossing the short end of a field still with the stone wall on your right and gorse to your left. In 30 paces bear left up the slope and then shortly left leaving the fenceline to pass through a gorse covered area with a little house away to your right.

A clear trackway is joined near the buildings at Pen-y-mynydd and this is followed through the gorse and rough pasture beyond which lie the conifers of Coed Cwm. Continue with the gated track passing the buildings

MAP 16/2

of Bodlonfa well away to your right and on to meet a minor road.

Turn left and follow the road for well over ¹/₂ mile with Coed Cwm to your left. Shortly after the woodland falls back turn right over a stile and go ahead with the boundary to your right. At the end of the field turn left along the edge and in 20 paces cross a stile and continue forward with the fence to your right. In a few steps bear slight diagonally left crossing the field to meet a stile on a minor road (nearly ¹/₂ mile east of Bwlch).

Cross the lane to the stile opposite and bear half left over the field towards the houses of Marian Cwm to a stile to cross a rough lane. Go forward to a further stile and up a hedged path between houses crossing a stile in a stone wall to meet the road opposite Hebor Cottage and the chapel of 1863.

Cross the road and go forward on a grassy lane to a stile, the chapel it will be seen has now been converted to a private residence not the only such change of use seen along the ODP. Bear half left up the hillside passing through a once quarried area. Soon a waymark post at top of a bank directs you forward. The path is narrow and at times indistinct as you climb north-westerly. At a further bank go forward to a level area with a waymark ahead, a view to the sea with a scatter of farms and hamlets dotted over the hills.

The ODP descends gently towards a small disused quarry pit, with the rocky slopes of Y Foel seen away to your left. Limestone quarries here have reduced the hill fort of Moel Hiraddug which stretched along the ridge but excavations in the nineteenth century produced evidence of a battle sometime before AD100.

From the old pit bear half left descending in the direction of the farm at Tyddyn-y-cyll to cross a stile at an angle of a stone wall. Go left over the stone stile and forward to a farm gate and stile, where turn left on a track to pass the farm.

About 100 yards beyond the farm turn right over a further stone stile descending on a grassy track to a ladder stile. Bear left to cross a further stile and turn right on a farm track to meet the road by Morwylfa. Turn left and almost immediately right over a stile and slight left over the field to meet the hedge and continue with this on your right. Cross a stile at the foot of a field to remain with the boundary to your right and over a short field to a stile to meet and turn right on a bridleway near Bryn Cnewyllyn.

Follow the gated way, passing a former waterworks and reservoir. At a junction with a lane by a house called Felin Fawr, turn left, crossing a stream and passing the Marian Mill trout hatchery to meet a minor road at a hairpin bend.

Go forward with the road, ie. right, for about 300 yards. As the road swings to the right leave it to cross a stile found on the left and over the field with a (perhaps temporary) wire fence to your right to meet the A5151 close to the farm at Ty Newydd.

Go over the road to a stile and then bear diagonally left to the hedge line then rising to a stile and over the next field slight diagonally left to meet a gateway and road on which turn left.

In 200 yards cross the stile on the right and up a stepped path to go forward to the top of a field. Beyond the stile bear slightly left to a stile and gap in the fence line and maintain your direction to a further stile. Continue over the field with a bungalow seen beyond the hedge to your left to a further stile to meet a lane.

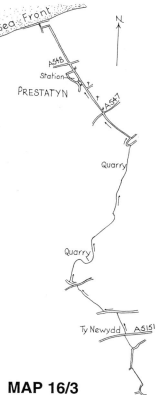

MAP 16/3

Bear left and in a few yards right at a junction. In a few yards more turn right on a metalled track passing through the gateway of Red Roofs. Just short of the house bear right to pass through a kissing gate to follow a hedged path, soon climbing with waymarked posts to meet a Y-junction. Take the left fork under the trees then a narrow path through gorse to emerge into the open with a view to the flat coastal strip and its thousands of retirement homes. Here too was the place of millions of holidays based on the caravan parks and holiday camps that developed along the coast from the 1930s.

As you reach the top of a deep quarry bear right on a narrow path soon passing through a kissing gate. Keep the quarry to your left throughout. When the path divides at a Y-junction ignore the left fork which descends to the foot of the quarry. Continue on the wider path through woodland, turn left to follow the far side of the quarry edged with orchids and views to the coastline.

The well waymarked path climbs through rough scrubland and gorse with

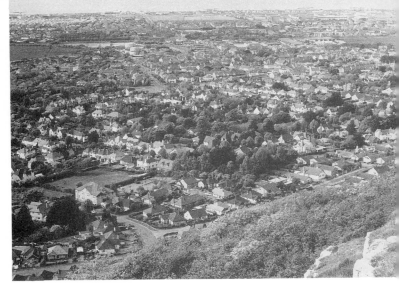

Journey's end - a very different view Prestatyn from the ODP

the earthworks of the twentieth century, a golf course, far below. When a crossing path is met do not descend but go ahead climbing to the last high viewpoint, about 650 feet.

The terraced path opens out to the final view of this long trek through the border country of England and Wales: not to the, often remote, rolling hills and forest but a return to today's civilisation with a gull's eye view of Prestatyn with its neatly laid out lines of white painted, red roofed houses, gasholder, station and hotels.

A gradual descent steepens, following the cliff edge of old quarries noisy with whirling jackdaws. On meeting the road, turn left and bear right round a hairpin bend to meet Bishops Wood Road, where turn right then curve left descending to cross the main road, then go forward down the High Street, passing the Scala Cinema which houses the Tourist Information Centre, and thence to the railway station with Offa's Tavern perhaps your journeys end.

To fully complete the coast to coast journey cross the station footbridge and go ahead on Bastion Road for ½ mile to meet the seafront with its caravan and campsites, amusement arcades and sandy beaches: a very different world from Offa's great frontier dyke which we have followed as it rolled across the hills and valleys from Severn shore to the blue/grey waters of the Irish Sea.

17: Useful Information

MAPS

1:50,000 Landranger Sheets (south to north)
  162 Gloucester and the Forest of Dean
  161 Abergavenny & the Black Mountains
  148 Presteigne and Hay-on-Wye
  137 Ludlow and Wenlock Edge
  126 Shrewsbury
  117 Chester and Wrexham
  116 Denbigh and Colwyn Bay

1:25,000 Outdoor Leisure Maps

Two of these excellent maps cover early sections of the walk and are included in preference to the Pathfinder series. The first opens up many miles of all-seasons walking between the Wye and Severn in the increasingly popular Forest of Dean. The second covers a wide area of the Black Mountains with much upland walking to be enjoyed between Abergavenny and Crickhowell in the south to Talgarth and Hay-on-Wye in the north.

Outdoor Leisure Map 14. Wye Valley and Forest of Dean
  Pathfinder   1087 (SO 41/51) Monmouth
           1086 (SO 21/31) Abergavenny
           1063 (SO 22/32) Longtown & Pandy

Outdoor Leisure Map 13. Brecon Beacons Eastern Area
  Pathfinder   1039 (SO 23/33) Golden Valley
           1016 (SO 24/34) Hay-on-Wye
           993 (SO 25/35) Kington
           971 (SO 26/36) Presteigne
           950 (SO 27/37) Knighton & Brampton Bryan
           930 (SO 28/38) Bishops Castle & Clun
           909 (SO 29/39) Montgomery
           888 (SJ 20/30) Welshpool
           868 (SJ 21/31) Middletown & Nesscliff

847 (SJ 22/32) Oswestry (South)
927 (SJ 23/33) Chirk & Ellesmere
806 (SJ 24/34) Llangollen & Wrexham (South)
789 (SJ 25/35) Wrexham (North)
772 (SJ 06/16) Denbigh
788 (SJ 05/15) Ruthin
755 (SJ 07/17) Holywell & St Asaph
737 (SJ 08/18) Rhyl

This long list of the larger scale maps may represent an expensive investment in total. It should be noted that some sheets may not be strictly necessary for your purpose and others may include only a small section of the ODP. The generally excellent waymarking of the route may serve to keep your reliance on maps to the 1:50,000 series.

TOURIST INFORMATION OFFICES

Note some may only have seasonal opening.

(south to north)

CHEPSTOW	Bridge Street, Chepstow NP6 5LH Tel: 01291 623772
MONMOUTH	Shire Hall, Agincourt Square, Monmouth NP5 3DY Tel: 01600 713899
ABERGAVENNY	Swan Meadow, Cross Street, Abergavenny NP7 5HH Tel: 01873 857588
HAY-ON-WYE	Craft Centre (main car park), Oxford Road, Hay-on-Wye HR3 5AE Tel: 01497 820144
KINGTON	2 Mill Street, Kington, Herefordshire Tel: 01544 230778
KNIGHTON	Offa's Dyke Centre, The Old School, West Street, Knighton LD7 1EW Tel: 01547 528753

WELSHPOOL	Flash Leisure Centre, Welshpool SY21 7DD
	Tel: 01938 552043
OSWESTRY	Mile End Services, Oswestry SY11 4JA
	Tel: 01691 662488
LLANGOLLEN	Town Hall, Castle Street, Llangollen LL20 5PD
	Tel: 01978 860828
RUTHIN	Craft Centre, Park Road, Ruthin LL15 1BB
	Tel: 01824 703992
PRESTATYN	Scala Cinema, High Street, Prestatyn LL19 9LH
	Tel: 01745 854365

TRAVEL

Rail
There are British Rail Stations which are on or within reasonable distance of the route at Chepstow, Abergavenny, Knighton, Welshpool, Ruabon, Wrexham and Prestatyn.

Coach
For National Express refer to your local yellow pages or nearest depot.

Local Bus Services
These can be very thin or non-existent in rural areas and any attempt to provide detailed information in a book is likely to become out of date very quickly. Sources of reference for the latest services are listed below.

WYE VALLEY AREA	Red and White (enquiries Chepstow (01291) 622947) provide services between Chepstow and Monmouth via Tintern.

OSWESTRY AREA	Midland Red (01691 652402) provide services Shrewsbury to Welshpool via Buttington. Oswestry/Trefonen/ Llanymynech. Oswestry/ Shrewsbury. Oswestry - Chirk - Wrexham. Crosville, Mold (01352 700250) Wrexham - Chester - Mold Llangollen, Trevor, Ruabon. Clwyd Bus (01352 704035) Shropshire Travel (01345 056785)
POWYS	Timetables and Powys Bus & Rail Guides can be supplied free of charge, stamped addressed envelope required, from Dept of Highways and Planning, Powys CC, County Hall, Llandrindod Wells, or inspected at libraries, Tourist Information Offices etc. A useful map which shows the Offa's Dyke Path lists operators and includes parts of Shropshire and Hereford & Worcester.
CLWYD	The County Council publishes a public transport guide with a map showing routes, some of which cross Offa's Dyke Path, with a list of operators. Timetables from Shire Hall, Mold or by phone 01352 752121 Ext 4035.

ACCOMMODATION

There is a good selection of accommodation in the main towns and larger villages. Despite the sometimes remote character of the Offa's Dyke Path there are surprisingly large numbers of bed and breakfasts on offer on or close to the route with not a few signed on stiles and gates. Tourist Information Offices are invariably helpful with up-to-date details on many types of accommodation. The Monmouth office for example has a list of accommodation on the route between Chepstow and Monmouth. A very useful booklet listing accommodation possibilities is published annually by the

Bunk house barn signing near Tremeirchion

Offa's Dyke Association which can be obtained from their HQ at The Old School, West Street, Knighton, Powys LD7 1EW (01547 528753). It is also stocked by the Ramblers' Association, 1/5 Wandsworth Road, London SW8 2LJ.

Youth Hostels

If you are not already a member this may be the time to join, membership applications to YHA, 8, St Stephen's Hill, St Albans. Herts. AL1 2DY. Tel: 01727 55215. Hostels on or near the route will be found at St Briavels, Monmouth, Capel-y-ffin, Knighton, Clun Mill, Llangollen and Maeshafn.

PLACES OF INTEREST

(south to north)

Times quoted are for guidance only and may be subject to change.

CHEPSTOW
Castle	Daily from 9.30, Sundays from 2pm
Museum	Daily March to October Mondays-Saturdays 11am-1pm 2-5pm. July to September 10.30am-5.30pm

St Marys Church	Daily

TINTERN

Abbey	Daily from 9.30, closes 4pm in winter, 7pm in summer
	Sundays from 2pm
The Old Station	Visitor Centre. Daily April to October 10.30am-5.30pm

MONMOUTH

Nelson Museum	Daily 10am-5pm, closes for lunch
	Sundays from 2pm

Castle and Regimental Museum
	Summer 2-5pm
	Winter Weekends 2-5pm

LLANTILIO CROSSENNY

The White Castle	Daily

LLANTHONY

Priory	Daily. Picnic site etc
St Davids Church	Daily

CAPEL-Y-FFIN

St Marys Church	Daily
Llanthony Abbey	Daily

HAY-ON-WYE

Secondhand book centre Daily

KINGTON

Hergest Croft Gardens	Late March to late October 1.30-6.30pm
Museum	Daily March to September. Winter Mondays, Wednesdays, Fridays from 10.30am

Oaklands Small Breeds Farm, Kingswood Kington
	Daily Good Friday to end October 10.30am-5.30pm

KNIGHTON
Offa's Dyke Association Visitor Centre, West Street

CLUN
Castle ruins   Daily, open access

MONTGOMERY
Castle   Daily

Museum   April to end September Saturdays and Bank Holidays 10.30am-5pm Wednesdays, Thursdays, Fridays and Sundays 1.30-5pm

WELSHPOOL
Powis Castle (NT) includes Robert Clive galleries

           Opening times vary during a long season but generally not Mondays and not Tuesdays early and late season. Grounds 11am-6pm and Castle 12-6pm

Powysland Museum and Canal Centre (Powys CC)

           Winter Mondays, Tuesdays, Thursdays and Fridays 11am-1pm & 2-5pm Saturdays 2-5pm Summer also Saturdays and Sundays 10am-5pm, closed for lunch

Moors Collection (Waterfowl, birds and rare breeds)

           A483 Welshpool Oswestry Road. Easter to mid October, closed Tuesdays and Wednesdays, daily July to August 10.30am-6pm

Welshpool and Llanfair Light Railway (01938 810 441)

           Early April to early October

LLANYMYNECH
Heritage Centre in quarry (informal). Nature trail

           Llanymynech Hill

WHITTINGTON
Castle   2 miles east of Oswestry. Daily
Park Hall Working Farm Museum
                                May to October daily except Fridays,
                                from 10am

OSWESTRY
Transport and Bicycle Museum
                                Daily 10am-4pm
Old Oswestry Hill Fort
                                1 mile north of Oswestry. Daily
Old Grammar School Heritage Centre
                                Daily except Sundays in winter

CHIRK
Castle (NT)   April to September daily except
                                Mondays and Saturdays
                                October Saturdays and Sundays only.
                                Castle 12-5pm Grounds 12-6pm

LLANGOLLEN
Plas Newydd   Open daily from April to October from
                                10am
Valle Crucis Abbey (near Llangollen)
                                Daily
Eliseg's Pillar   B5105 north of abbey open access
Castell Dinas Bran   Open access
Motor Museum   Daily Easter to October from 10am.
                                Winter Mondays to Fridays from 10am
Llangollen Railway   Daily April to October
Horsedrawn barge trips from Llangollen Wharf
                                Easter to September
                                Canal exhibition on wharf

DENBIGH
Castle   Daily

ERDDIG (near Wrexham) (N.T.)

House and garden April to early October daily except Thursdays and Fridays. House 12-5pm. Gardens from 11am

ST ASAPH
Cathedral   Daily

RHUDDLAN
Castle   Daily

*   *   *

APPENDIX A: MILEAGE CHART

Mileage	Suggested Route	Official Route
Sedbury Cliffs to Monmouth		$17^{1/4}$
Chepstow to Monmouth	$16^{1/2}$	
Monmouth to Pandy	$16^{3/4}$	$16^{3/4}$
Pandy to Hay-on-Wye	$17^{3/4}$	17
Hay-on-Wye to Kington	$14^{1/4}$	$14^{1/4}$
Kington to Knighton	14	14
Knighton to Newcastle	$8^{1/4}$	
Excluding stopover Newcastle		$7^{3/4}$
Newcastle to Montgomery	$11^{1/4}$	$9^{3/4}$
Montgomery to Buttington (for Welshpool)		$10^{3/4}$
Montgomery to Welshpool	14	
Buttington to Llanymynech		$10^{1/4}$
Welshpool to Llanymynech	$12^{1/4}$	
Llanymynech to Tyn-y-Coed		$6^{1/4}$
Llanymynech to Oswestry	$8^{3/4}$	
Oswestry to Llangollen	$17^{1/2}$	
Oswestry to Llangollen via Dinas Bran		15
Trevor Rocks to Pen-y-stryt		$7^{1/4}$
Llangollen to Pen-y-stryt	$8^{1/2}$	
Pen-y-stryt to Bwlch Penbarra	$8^{1/2}$	$8^{1/2}$
Bwlch Penbarra to Bodfari	$8^{3/4}$	$8^{3/4}$
Bodfari to Prestatyn	$11^{1/2}$	$11^{1/2}$
TOTALS	$188^{1/2}$	175

All mileages quoted are approximate

CICERONE GUIDES

Cicerone publish a wide range of reliable guides to walking and climbing abroad

FRANCE, BELGIUM & LUXEMBOURG
CHAMONIX MONT BLANC - A Walking Guide
THE CORSICAN HIGH LEVEL ROUTE: GR20
FRENCH ROCK
THE PYRENEAN TRAIL: GR10
THE RLS (Stevenson) TRAIL
ROCK CLIMBS IN BELGIUM & LUXEMBOURG
ROCK CLIMBS IN THE VERDON
TOUR OF MONT BLANC
TOUR OF THE OISANS: GR54
TOUR OF THE QUEYRAS
WALKING THE FRENCH ALPS: GR5
WALKING THE FRENCH GORGES (Provence)
WALKS IN VOLCANO COUNTRY (Auvergne)
THE WAY OF ST JAMES: GR65

FRANCE / SPAIN
WALKS AND CLIMBS IN THE PYRENEES
ROCK CLIMBS IN THE PYRENEES

SPAIN
ANDALUSIAN ROCK CLIMBS
BIRDWATCHING IN MALLORCA
COSTA BLANCA CLIMBS
MOUNTAIN WALKS ON THE COSTA BLANCA
WALKING IN MALLORCA
WALKS & CLIMBS IN THE PICOS DE EUROPA
THE WAY OF ST JAMES: SPAIN

FRANCE / SWITZERLAND
CHAMONIX TO ZERMATT The Walker's Haute Route
THE JURA - Walking the High Route and Winter Ski
  Traverses

SWITZERLAND
THE ALPINE PASS ROUTE
THE BERNESE ALPS
CENTRAL SWITZERLAND
WALKS IN THE ENGADINE
WALKING IN TICINO
THE VALAIS - A Walking Guide

GERMANY / AUSTRIA / EASTERN EUROPE
HUT-TO-HUT IN THE STUBAI ALPS
THE HIGH TATRAS
THE KALKALPEN TRAVERSE
KING LUDWIG WAY
KLETTERSTEIG - Scrambles
MOUNTAIN WALKING IN AUSTRIA
WALKING IN THE BLACK FOREST
WALKING IN THE HARZ MOUNTAINS
WALKING IN THE SALZKAMMERGUT

ITALY & SLOVENIA
ALTA VIA - High Level Walks in the Dolomites
CLASSIC CLIMBS IN THE DOLOMITES
ITALIAN ROCK - Rock Climbs in Northern Italy
VIA FERRATA - Scrambles in the Dolomites
WALKING IN THE DOLOMITES
WALKS IN THE JULIAN ALPS

MEDITERRANEAN COUNTRIES
THE ATLAS MOUNTAINS
CRETE: Off the beaten track
THE MOUNTAINS OF GREECE
THE MOUNTAINS OF TURKEY
TREKS & CLIMBS IN WADI RUM, JORDAN
THE ALA DAG - Climbs & Treks (Turkey)

OTHER COUNTRIES
ADVENTURE TREKS - W. N. AMERICA
ANNAPURNA TREKKERS GUIDE
CLASSIC TRAMPS IN NEW ZEALAND
MOUNTAIN WALKING IN AFRICA 1: KENYA
ROCK CLIMBING IN HONG KONG
TREKKING IN THE CAUCAUSUS
TREKKING IN NEPAL
TREKKING - WESTERN NORTH AMERICA

GENERAL OUTDOOR BOOKS
THE ADVENTURE ALTERNATIVE
FIRST AID FOR HILLWALKERS
THE HILL WALKERS MANUAL
LIMESTONE -100 BEST CLIMBS IN BRITAIN
MOUNTAIN WEATHER
MOUNTAINEERING LITERATURE
MODERN ALPINE CLIMBING
MODERN SNOW & ICE TECHNIQUES
ROPE TECHNIQUES IN MOUNTAINEERING

CANOEING
CANOEIST'S GUIDE TO THE NORTH EAST
SNOWDONIA WILD WATER, SEA & SURF
WILDWATER CANOEING

CARTOON BOOKS
ON FOOT & FINGER
ON MORE FEET & FINGERS
LAUGHS ALONG THE PENNINE WAY
THE WALKERS

*Also a full range of guidebooks
to walking, scrambling, ice-climbing,
rock climbing, and other adventurous
pursuits in Britain and abroad*

*Other guides are constantly being added to the Cicerone List.
Available from bookshops, outdoor equipment shops or direct (send for price list)
from CICERONE, 2 POLICE SQUARE, MILNTHORPE, CUMBRIA, LA7 7PY*

CICERONE GUIDES
Cicerone publish a wide range of reliable guides to walking and climbing in Britain, and other general interest books.

LAKE DISTRICT - General Books
CONISTON COPPER A History
CHRONICLES OF MILNTHORPE
A DREAM OF EDEN
THE HIGH FELLS OF LAKELAND
LAKELAND - A taste to remember (Recipes)
LAKELAND VILLAGES
LAKELAND TOWNS
THE LOST RESORT? (Morecambe)
LOST LANCASHIRE (Furness area)
OUR CUMBRIA Stories of Cumbrian Men and Women
THE PRIORY OF CARTMEL
REFLECTIONS ON THE LAKES
AN ILLUSTRATED COMPANION INTO LAKELAND

LAKE DISTRICT - Guide Books
THE BORDERS OF LAKELAND
BIRDS OF MORECAMBE BAY
CASTLES IN CUMBRIA
CONISTON COPPER MINES Field Guide
THE CUMBRIA CYCLE WAY
THE EDEN WAY
IN SEARCH OF WESTMORLAND
SHORT WALKS IN LAKELND-1: SOUTH LAKELAND
SCRAMBLES IN THE LAKE DISTRICT
MORE SCRAMBLES IN THE LAKE DISTRICT
WALKING ROUND THE LAKES
WALKS IN SILVERDALE/ARNSIDE
WESTMORLAND HERITAGE WALK
WINTER CLIMBS IN THE LAKE DISTRICT

NORTHERN ENGLAND (outside the Lakes
BIRDWATCHING ON MERSEYSIDE
CANAL WALKS Vol 1 North
CANOEISTS GUIDE TO THE NORTH EAST
THE CLEVELAND WAY & MISSING LINK
THE DALES WAY
DOUGLAS VALLEY WAY
WALKING IN THE FOREST OF BOWLAND
HADRIANS WALL Vol 1 The Wall Walk
HERITAGE TRAILS IN NW ENGLAND
THE ISLE OF MAN COASTAL PATH
IVORY TOWERS & DRESSED STONES (Follies)
THE LANCASTER CANAL
LANCASTER CANAL WALKS
A WALKERS GUIDE TO THE LANCASTER CANAL
LAUGHS ALONG THE PENNINE WAY
A NORTHERN COAST-TO-COAST
NORTH YORK MOORS Walks
THE REIVERS WAY (Northumberland)
THE RIBBLE WAY
ROCK CLIMBS LANCASHIRE & NW
WALKING DOWN THE LUNE
WALKING IN THE SOUTH PENNINES
WALKING IN THE NORTH PENNINES
WALKING IN THE WOLDS
WALKS IN THE YORKSHIRE DALES (3 VOL)
WALKS IN LANCASHIRE WITCH COUNTRY
WALKS IN THE NORTH YORK MOORS
WALKS TO YORKSHIRE WATERFALLS (2 vol)
WATERFALL WALKS -TEESDALE & THE HIGH PENNINES
WALKS ON THE WEST PENNINE MOORS
WALKING NORTHERN RAILWAYS (2 vol)
THE YORKSHIRE DALES A walker's guide

Also a full range of EUROPEAN and OVERSEAS guidebooks - walking, long distance trails, scrambling, ice-climbing, rock climbing.

DERBYSHIRE & EAST MIDLANDS
KINDER LOG
HIGH PEAK WALKS
WHITE PEAK WAY
WHITE PEAK WALKS - 2 Vols
WEEKEND WALKS IN THE PEAK DISTRICT
THE VIKING WAY
THE DEVIL'S MILL / WHISTLING CLOUGH (Novels)

WALES & WEST MIDLANDS
ASCENT OF SNOWDON
WALKING IN CHESHIRE
CLWYD ROCK
HEREFORD & THE WYE VALLEY A Walker's Guide
HILLWALKING IN SNOWDONIA
HILL WALKING IN WALES (2 Vols)
THE MOUNTAINS OF ENGLAND & WALES Vol 1 WALES
WALKING OFFA'S DYKE PATH
THE RIDGES OF SNOWDONIA
ROCK CLIMBS IN WEST MIDLANDS
SARN HELEN Walking Roman Road
SCRAMBLES IN SNOWDONIA
SNOWDONIA WHITE WATER SEA & SURF
THE SHROPSHIRE HILLS A Walker's Guide
WALKING DOWN THE WYE
WELSH WINTER CLIMBS

SOUTH & SOUTH WEST ENGLAND
WALKING IN THE CHILTERNS
COTSWOLD WAY
COTSWOLD WAY (3 VOLS)
WALKING ON DARTMOOR
WALKERS GUIDE TO DARTMOOR PUBS
EXMOOR & THE QUANTOCKS
THE KENNET & AVON WALK
LONDON THEME WALKS
AN OXBRIDGE WALK
A SOUTHERN COUNTIES BIKE GUIDE
THE SOUTHERN-COAST-TO-COAST
SOUTH DOWNS WAY & DOWNS LINK
SOUTH WEST WAY - 2 Vol
THE TWO MOORS WAY Dartmoor-Exmoor
WALKS IN KENT Bk 2
THE WEALDWAY & VANGUARD WAY

SCOTLAND
THE BORDER COUNTRY - WALKERS GUIDE
BORDER PUBS & INNS A Walker's Guide
CAIRNGORMS WINTER CLIMBS
WALKING THE GALLOWAY HILLS
THE ISLAND OF RHUM
THE SCOTTISH GLENS (Mountainbike Guide)
   Book 1:THE CAIRNGORM GLENS
   Book 2 THE ATHOLL GLENS
   Book 3 THE GLENS OF RANNOCH
SCOTTISH RAILWAY WALKS
SCRAMBLES IN LOCHABER
SCRAMBLES IN SKYE
SKI TOURING IN SCOTLAND
TORRIDON A Walker's Guide
WALKS from the WEST HIGHLAND RAILWAY
WINTER CLIMBS BEN NEVIS & GLENCOE

REGIONAL BOOKS UK & IRELAND
THE ALTERNATIVE PENNINE WAY
CANAL WALKS Vol.1: North
LIMESTONE - 100 BEST CLIMBS
THE PACKHORSE BRIDGES OF ENGLAND
THE RELATIVE HILLS OF BRITAIN
THE MOUNTAINS OF ENGLAND & WALES
   VOL 1 WALES,   VOL 2 ENGLAND
THE MOUNTAINS OF IRELAND

Other guides are constantly being added to the Cicerone List.
Available from bookshops, outdoor equipment shops or direct (send s.a.e. for price list) from
CICERONE, 2 POLICE SQUARE, MILNTHORPE, CUMBRIA, LA7 7PY

TEXT PRINTED BY ST EDMUNDSBURY PRESS, BURY ST EDMUNDS